INESS
STRATION

NVQ
LEVEL 1

Val Warrilow

HEINEMANN

Heinemann Educational,
a division of Heinemann Publishers (Oxford) Ltd
Halley Court, Jordan Hill, Oxford OX2 8 EJ

Oxford   London   Edinburgh
Madrid   Athens   Bologna   Paris
Melbourne   Sydney   Auckland
Singapore   Tokyo   Ibadan   Nairobi
Harare   Gaborone   Portsmouth NH (USA)

A catalogue record for this book is available
from the British Library on request.

ISBN 0435 45009 3

Designed and produced by Ken Vail Graphic Design, Cambridge

Printed and bound by Bath Press, Avon, England

Contents

1 Filing   5
1.1 File documents and open new files within an established filing system   5
1.2 Identify and retrieve documents from within an established filing system   13

2 Communicating information   17
2.1 Process incoming and outgoing business telephone calls   17
2.2 Receive and relay oral and written messages   26
2.3 Supply information for a specific purpose   30
2.4 Draft routine business communications   35

3 Data processing   47
3.1 Produce alpha/numerical information in typewritten form   47
3.2 Identify and mark errors on scripted material, for correction   54
3.3 Update records in a computerised database   58

4 Processing petty cash and invoices   64
4.1 Process petty cash transactions   64
4.2 Process incoming invoices for payment   70

5 Stock handling   76
5.1 Issue office materials on request and monitor stock levels   76

6 Mail handling   86
6.1 Receive, sort and distribute incoming/internal mail   86
6.2 Prepare for despatch outgoing/internal mail   90

7 Reprographics   98
7.1 Produce copies from original documents using reprographic equipment   98

8 Liaising with callers and colleagues   106
8.1 Receive and assist callers   106
8.2 Maintain business relationships with other members of staff   112

9 Health and safety   116
9.1 Operate safely in the workplace   116

10 Applying for a job   122

11 The interview   125

Key to activities   127

Photocopiable sheets   147

Index   158

1 Filing

1.1 File documents and open new files within an established filing system

This section covers

- documents for filing
- sorting documents
- filing systems
- filing equipment
- safety
- preparing new files
- indexing systems
- cross-referencing
- confidential files.
- bulky or completed files
- document retention.

Why file?

'I had it in my hand only a minute ago, Mrs Pearson!'

- Up-to-date information can be found *immediately*.
- Queries can be answered quickly and efficiently.
- Time is not wasted searching through piles of unfiled documents.

Documents for filing

Make a list of all the various types of documents which you could be asked to file in an office. Can you think of at least *five* different types? Compare your list with the other members of your group.

It is important that papers are not filed away before they have been dealt with. To show that documents have been released for filing, a special mark called a **release symbol** is marked on them. A tick, initials or a large 'F' for 'File' could all be used.

Sorting documents

It saves time if documents are pre-sorted before putting them away in the filing cabinets. A useful aid is a **desk sorter** which is made up of a number of heavy 'pages' each labelled with a letter of the alphabet. Papers can then be placed behind each appropriate page.

After sorting, holes are punched in the documents so they can be attached securely inside the files. Make sure that holes are punched squarely by aligning the centre arrow on the punch with the middle of the document *or* by using the alignment guide on the punch. *Never guess!*

Filing systems

Documents are filed away in order so that they can easily be found again. Most organisations use either an **alphabetical** system or a **numerical** system of classification.

Alphabetical

This is the system most widely used because it is easy for people to operate. However, there are several rules to remember:

Names of individuals

1 File under first letter of surname ----------------------**K**han, Farida
   Parker, Jason
2 Short before long --------------------------------------Brown before Browne
3 When surname is same, --------------------------------Thompson, **A**lice
   follow first name or initials   Thompson, **L**orraine
   Thompson, **W**illiam
4 Initials before full name --------------------------------Lucas, **B**
   Lucas, **B T**
   Lucas, **Brian**
5 Mac and Mc – all treated as Mac – file before 'M' -**McA**dam, A
   MacDowell, A
   Mason, A
6 Ignore apostrophes --------------------------------------**O**Brien (O'Brien)

Names of organisations

1 Public bodies filed under name or town -------------**P**reston County Council
   Social Security, Dept of
2 Ignore the word 'The' -----------------------------------**C**atering Centre, The
   Pines Hotel, The
3 Saint and St – all treated as Saint
4 Initials in company names filed -----------------------**RTL** Engineering plc
   at the beginning of section   **Ra**thbone & Company
5 Treat numbers as word
   e.g. 1st Class Paint Company ---------------------------**F**irst Class Paint Company

If you are unsure about the alphabetical order of files, check the order of the telephone directory – it is an excellent guide!

Referring to the rules listed above, write out the following names in strict *alphabetical* order. Put the surname first as shown in the example.

		Example
Julian McIvor	Robert Black	Adams, R & Co Ltd
7-day Service Company	St Thomas' Nursery	Adamson, Paul
Pauline Clark	R Black	
The Bread Shop	Paul Adamson	
Peter Clarke	Department of the Environment	
Greengage Hotel	R Adams & Co Ltd	
VDU Sales Ltd	Trevor Green	
Vintage Wine Company	Charles Samuel	

Numerical

A numerical system is very easy to follow but a separate index must be kept of names in alphabetical order. The file number can quickly be found by checking the alphabetical index.

Rearrange the following list into *numerical* order.

Follow the example shown.

Barker, A	– 74723	Bickley, M	– 77593	
Barton, T	– 77472	Bodworth, R	– 76241	
Battersby, W	– 75231	Boston, L	– 7621	
Belling, S	– 7249	Botham, D	– 7543	
Bentley, P	– 731	Bottomly, R	– 77571	
Berry, K	– 74256	Burgess, D	– 73814	

Example

731 – P Bentley
7249 – S Belling

Smithson, C 5823
Smith, A 3562

Take care not to copy figures incorrectly!

There are other filing systems which are sometimes used. These are
- **chronological** – filing by date
- **geographical** – filing by area
- **subject** – filing by topic

Often, documents are filed using *two* classifications; the main system could be in **alphabetical** order but within each individual file, the documents are filed in **date** order.

Filing equipment

There are *four* main methods of filing documents.

Vertical
- Metal cabinets with two, three, or four drawers
- Usually files are kept in suspended pockets
- Labels are placed on top of suspended pocket
- Cabinets can be supplied in a variety of colours

Lateral
- Cabinets with shelves with files stored side by side
- Files suspended in pockets
- Labels placed on side of pocket
- Other shelves in cabinet can be used for other types of storage

Horizontal
- Chest containing shallow drawers for storing plans, photographs
- Labels placed on front of drawer showing contents

Rotary
- Files suspended in pockets on a revolving stand
- Gives all round access
- Labels placed on side of pocket

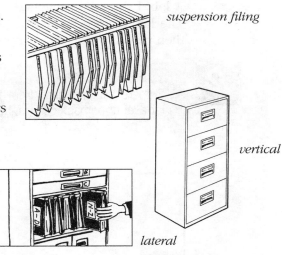

suspension filing

vertical

lateral

horizontal

rotary

Safety

! **Never** leave filing cabinet drawers open. People can walk into them. (Modern cabinets will not allow more than one drawer at a time to open.)

! **Always** use a proper filing stool, or steps, to reach high shelves – **never** a swivel chair.

! Cabinets are usually made of metal – this will give documents a limited amount of protection in the event of fire.

! Do not place cabinets too near doors.

Preparing new files

Filed papers are usually kept in a **wallet folder** or can be fastened inside a **manilla folder** to prevent them becoming lost.

wallet

manilla

A **label** should be attached to the outside of each file clearly showing the title. The label can be typed or boldly handwritten with black pen. The folder is then placed inside the suspended pocket of the filing cabinet.

Your tutor will give you *two* sheets illustrating the shape of files (page 147). Prepare two new files from the details shown below. You could use a stencil, letraset or perhaps calligraphy writing.

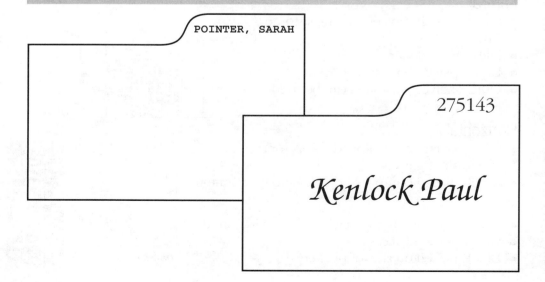

POINTER, SARAH

275143

Kenlock Paul

Indexing systems

Many organisations keep a **card index** of information as well as a file for the topic. As previously mentioned on page **7**, an alphabetical index would be necessary to locate files in a numerical system.

Additional information such as address, telephone number and date of birth is often kept on the index card.

Name JACKSON, IAN J	Number 472
Address 432 CLAREMONT ROAD NORTHAMPTON NN1 1LB	
Telephone No 0604 274318	Date of birth 24-10-65
Details Previous employment:	Blythe & Co Fenton St Northampton

Your tutor will give you *four* blank index cards (page 148). Complete each of these with the details given below. They can be either typewritten or handwritten neatly.

STEPHEN FOSTER
27 Canterbury Way
Bristol
BS98 4RG
Telephone 0272 576684
Date of birth 27.12.55
Number 3742

HANIF SHAIKH
48 Portland Street
Leicester
LE2 7DD
Telephone 0533 564739
Date of birth 14.09.60
Number 2832

PAULINE DIXON
49 Pringle Drive
Dunfermline
KY45 9KJ
Telephone 0383 463532
Date of birth 12.06.71
Number 2895

JOHN O'DRISCOLL
312 Devonport Road
Preston
PR5 2FG
Telephone 0772 465832
Date of birth 08.08.65
Number 3275

For additional practice, make out an index card for each member of your group. Allocate each member a reference number.

You will need to find out
• full name
• address and post code
• telephone number
• date of birth
• reference number.

Why not collect some additional details of each person such as previous school, hobbies etc, so you can make a note of these on each person's card?

Guillotine each card and practise sorting these into
• alphabetical order
• numerical order
• date of birth order.

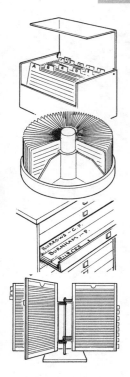

Index cards can be stored in a number of ways.

Card index box
- Cards are filed one behind the other, separated by guide cards to assist identification.
- The box can be kept on a desk for quick, easy access.

Rotary index
- Cards are stored in a rotating wheel, enabling the user to see information at a glance.
- Cards can be taken out or added to with ease.

Visible edge index
- Cards are laid out in flat drawers with the title visible at the bottom of the cards.
- Cards can be updated without removing them from the tray.
- Coloured markers on the edge of each card can help identification.

Strip index
- A large book with heavy pages contains strips instead of cards which can be added or removed easily.
- It is only possible to keep a limited amount of information on the strips but different colours can be used to identify topics.

Cross-referencing

Sometimes we look in a telephone directory or *Yellow Pages* for a particular number, only to find that we are directed to look elsewhere.

◆ **Motels**
SEE HOTELS AND INNS

● **Fashion Designers**
See Designers – Garments

◆ **Passport offices**
SEE ALSO POST OFFICES

This redirection is called **cross-referencing**.

Under which letters of the alphabet would you find the telephone numbers for the following?
- National Girobank
- British Gas
- National Blood Transfusion Service
- Job Centre
- Ministry of Pensions and National Insurance
- Royal Naval Establishments

Have you decided?

Now check with the telephone directory. See how you have been directed to the correct place by cross-referencing.

When preparing new files, if a topic could quite easily be filed under two different letters of the alphabet, we could make out a **cross-reference card** which would direct people to the place where the file was actually kept.

Cross-reference card
for
Time Computing
see COMPUTER SUPPLIES

Confidential files

In any company many files contain information which should not be available for others to see. For example in the Personnel Department, files may contain details of medical matters or criminal convictions.

Confidential files should be kept locked in a separate cabinet and only made available to those with the proper authority. They should *never* be left lying on a desk.

Bulky or completed files

Filing cabinets must be inspected at regular intervals – usually between three and six months.

If a topic has been completed, the file can be
- taken out but retained elsewhere (often in basement storage), *or*
- destroyed, if no longer required.

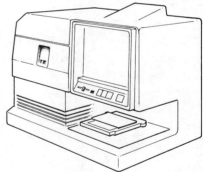

microfilm

microfiche

Most companies prefer to shred completed files to prevent unauthorised people reading them. Documents are fed into a **shredding machine** which cuts them into unreadable strips.

If a file is still **current** but needs to be thinned out, correspondence that has been in the file for more than a certain period of time (say three months) is taken out and transferred to long term storage.

Current files, however bulky, are *never* destroyed until the matter is completed.

Remember, new files cannot be added to cabinets unless some are first removed!

An alternative method of storing completed or bulky files is **microfilming**. Important documents are photographed and the negatives are kept in miniature form on either **film** or **fiche**.

A **reader** or **viewer** is needed to view the film or fiche. The images are enlarged and, if a **printer** is also incorporated, a photocopy of the required document can be taken.

reader/viewer with photocopier

It is possible that you have actually used a microfiche reader or seen one in use. Can you think where?

Document retention

Obviously it is not possible to keep *all* completed files indefinitely and the following guidelines should be observed.

Documents	keep for
Ordinary business correspondence	1 or 2 years
Accounts and VAT documents	minimum of 6 years (required by law)
Legal documents	minimum of 6 years (important documents should be kept indefinitely)

Section review

Can you identify the illustrations shown below? Choose from the list on the left of the page.

- File labels

- Punch

- Stapler

- Box file

- Ring binder

- Card index box

- Vertical cabinet

- Suspension filing

- Filing stool

- Wallet folder

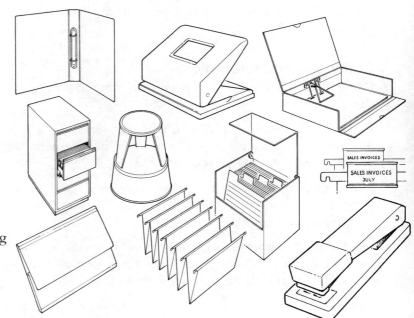

Complete the blank spaces in the following passage using each of the listed words once only.

suspended	vertical
alphabetical	numerical
confidential	index
release	cross-reference
microfiche	sorted

A _____ symbol is marked on all documents which are ready for filing. Before attempting to file documents, they should be _____ into some type of classification, usually _____ or _____. An _____ is always needed when using a numerical classification.

The most popular type of filing system is the _____ cabinet which consists of two, three or four drawers and files are usually kept in _____ pockets.

If a file could be placed under two letters of the alphabet, a _____ card should be made out.

Files which should only be seen by a limited number of people are referred to as _____ files.

To save space, important documents can be photographed and the negatives stored on _____ .

1.2 Identify and retrieve documents from within an established filing system

This section covers

- organisation of filing
  - centralised
  - departmental
- locating files

- booking in and out procedures
- delays in supplying files
- reminder systems and overdue files.

Organisation of filing

There are *two* main methods of organising files.

Centralised filing

All the company's filing is kept in one large area.

Advantages	Disadvantages
✔ Filing staff are competent and well-trained.	✘ Files are not always close to hand.
✔ Only one type of classification is used eg alphabetical, numerical.	✘ Delays can occur when answering telephone queries.
✔ Missing files are chased up regularly.	
✔ Cabinets and files are maintained in good order.	

Departmental filing

Each department has its own filing system within that department.

Advantages	Disadvantages
✔ Files can be referred to quickly.	✘ Departments may not use the same method of classification throughout the company.
	✘ More cabinets will be needed.
	✘ Staff may not be as competent at filing if other duties need to be done.

Organisations which operate a centralised system of filing often encourage individual departments to keep their own card index record for the people with whom they usually deal.

Can you think why this is so?

What sort of details would you suggest should be kept on each index card?

Locating files

Individual files often need to be taken from the filing cabinet, usually when further information on a particular topic is required.

This could be caused by
- a letter received containing an enquiry
- a personal caller to the office

- a telephone enquiry
- a reminder in the diary.

'Mrs Pearson – your time is up.'

Because files are continually needed for reference by various people, the following rules must be observed.

- All documents relating to the topic must be filed away regularly – daily, if possible.
- Individual documents or letters must *not* be taken out of a file – a photocopy of the item should be made instead.
- If a file needs to be borrowed, a note in the form of an absent card must be completed and placed where the file is usually kept.
- Files which have been borrowed for more than several days must be chased up and returned.

Booking in and out procedures

How many times have you looked in a cabinet for a file only to find that someone else has borrowed it? If you know the name of the person who has taken the file, then there is no problem.

A sensible filing clerk will make sure that no file is taken without an **absent (*or out*) card** being completed and placed where the file is usually kept. The absent card is completed with details of the file borrowed, name of borrower and date.

When the file is returned to the cabinet, the absent card is removed.

The absent card is put in the place of the borrowed file.

The filing drawers should be checked daily and files which have been borrowed and not returned within a reasonable period of time should be chased up for return.

Your tutor will give you an absent card (page 149). Complete this with the following details of files borrowed.

Cross through each entry if the file has been returned before moving on to the next.

1 Control Services plc file was borrowed on 3 February by Jane Mortimer of Accounts. She returned the file on 5 February.

2 Fatima Sidat of Purchasing took the file for Hamilton & Co on 7 February and returned it the same day.

3 On 9 February, the file for Key Business Systems was borrowed by Julie Carter of the Technical Department. She returned the file four days later.

4 The file for Mehmood Khan was borrowed by Gary Rogers of Personnel on 15 February and returned the day after.

5 Tony Wilkins of Sales took the file for Star Engineering plc on 21 February. The file has not yet been returned.

Delays in supplying files

Unfortunately, it is not always possible to supply a file immediately to the person requesting it.

Can you think of *three* reasons for this?

The delay could be because
- someone else is using the file
- the file is currently being updated
- the file has been put back in the wrong place!

Assume that your manager, Robert Kingsley, has requested a file for Mrs Janice Worden. An absent card informs you that this file was borrowed by Simon Boston from Accounts 2 days ago.

Write down exactly how you would explain to Mr Kingsley why you cannot let him have the file immediately and then state what action you will be taking to obtain the file for him.

Reminder systems and overdue files

Smaller offices will find that by checking the absent or out cards in the cabinet drawers periodically, this is sufficient to check whether files have been borrowed for an unreasonable length of time.

Larger organisations may
- keep a **returns diary** with the files listed under the **date of return**. Files will be crossed out when returned, leaving overdue files to be chased up.

- make out a card for each file borrowed and file it in a **card index box** under the **date of return**. The card is removed when the file is returned, leaving cards for outstanding files remaining in the box.

RETURNS DIARY	
DATE OF RETURN	FILE NAME
17/6/92	Johnson & Co
17/6/92	~~LONDON STEEL LTD,~~
18/6/92	~~Billingham Traders Ltd~~
18/6/92	Emersley Fabrics
18/6/92	~~MICROMART LTD~~

RETURN BY	FILE NAME
21/6/92	NIGHTINGALE LTD

RETURN BY	FILE NAME
18/6/92	EMERSLEY FABRICS

RETURN BY	FILE NAME
17/6/92	Johnson & Co

Section review

Fill in the missing letters and then write the completed words in your folder to help you remember them.

1 To ensure that holes are punched squarely, use the _l_gn___t guide on the punch.

2 A numerical filing system needs an __ph_b_____l index.

3 Two types of folder for holding documents are called __ll_t and m___lla.

4 It is usual to have s__p__s___ filing in vertical and lateral cabinets.

5 Where a file could be put in two different places, a ___ss-r__er__ce card should be used.

6 C__f_d__t___ files should never be left lying on a desk.

7 Depending upon the size of the organisation, filing may be centralised or __p_rt__nt__.

8 To indicate that a file has been borrowed, it is usual to complete an _u_ or __s__t card.

9 A r_m__d__ system should be kept to ensure that borrowed files are chased up.

10 As a __fe_y precaution, cabinets are made of metal.

Crossword

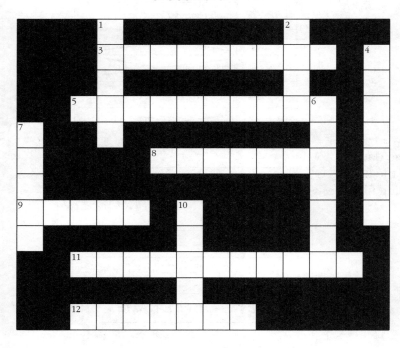

Across

3 A type of classification (9)
5 Is used before putting documents into filing cabinets (4) (6)
8 A type of filing cabinet (7)
9 A type of file which is retained indefinitely (5)
11 Files are kept in one place (11)
12 A file which has not been returned (7)

Down

1 Is required with a numerical classification (5)
2 A type of filing classification (4)
4 Must be done if a file is not returned (5) (2)
6 Mark to indicate that documents can be filed (7)
7 How often should filing be done? (5)
10 To destroy completed files (5)

2 Communicating information

2.1 Process incoming and outgoing business telephone calls

This section covers

- telephone systems
- telephone features
- answering the telephone
- making outgoing telephone calls
- confirming telephone arrangements
- answering machines
- telephone reference books
- telephone services
- telephone faults
- telephone charge rates
- security procedures and emergencies.

Message taking is covered in Section 2.2 page 26.

A large proportion of business today is conducted by **telephone**. Unfortunately, receiving and making telephone calls is probably one of the most dreaded jobs for the inexperienced office worker.

Fears can include
- disconnecting callers by accident
- not being able to transfer a call
- being unable to give the information requested
- having to deal with an angry caller
- getting a message muddled.

It is important therefore that you learn good telephone skills which will enable you to become more confident and efficient.

'I'm really getting the hang of this switchboard, Mrs Pearson. I've only cut seven callers off today.'

Telephone systems

The type of telephone system at your workplace will depend upon the size of your organisation.

Private Automatic Branch Exchange (PABX)

This switchboard will be manned by an operator who answers all incoming calls from a central location.

The operator will transfer calls to other extension users (sometimes well over 100 extensions).

Larger PABXs have **visual display units** (VDUs) enabling the operator to view the whole system on screen at one time.

Multiline or Key Telephone System (KTS)

This system allows all extensions to receive calls, *or* one extension only can act as the switchboard. Although up to 80 extensions can be accommodated, it is usual to have no more than about 25.

Telephone features

Many different features are available on modern telephones.

Redial button	Enables you to try the last dialled number again if you could not get through previously.
Liquid crystal display (LCD)	Shows the number you are dialling or recalling from memory on a small screen.
Memories	Frequently called numbers can be put into memory and recalled by pressing a couple of buttons.
Secrecy button	Allows you to speak to someone else in the room without your caller hearing. Just putting your hand over the receiver is not adequate!
Call timer/clock	A display on the phone shows how long each call lasts – useful for keeping costs down! The display acts as a clock when *not* used as a timer.
On-hook dialling	Dial a number – no need to lift the handset until someone answers.
Hands-free operation	A built-in microphone and adjustable loudspeaker allows you to hold a conversation without lifting the handset. Hands are kept free for making notes.
Prompt	If a number is engaged, the phone will store it and three minutes later will bleep to remind you to try it again.

TouchTone phones

If your BT telephone exchange has been modernised, you can have a TouchTone phone. TouchTone phones play notes when you dial.

Users have access to the following services for a small rental charge.

Charge advice	After finishing your call, replace the receiver. Your phone will ring and an electronic 'voice' will tell you the cost of the call.
Reminder call	You can book your own alarm call by pressing certain buttons. Calls can also be cancelled.
Call diversion	Your calls can automatically be transferred to another number.
Call waiting	Whilst you are on the phone, a discreet bleep will let you know that another caller is waiting. An option allows you to put your first call on hold whilst you answer the other one.
Three-way calling	Three callers, all on separate telephones, can hold a conversation.
Code calling	Up to 27 frequently called numbers can be stored and redialled by just pressing two buttons.
Repeat last call	Engaged numbers can be redialled automatically by pressing three buttons.

Answering the telephone

An incoming call can be
- received direct from an outside line
- transferred to you from your switchboard operator
- transferred to you from another extension.

The tone of the ring will help you to identify whether the call is from an outside line or another extension.

Calls from an outside line should be answered with a greeting and the name of your firm.

'Good morning, Sutcliffe & Jones, Solicitors'

When answering internal calls, your name, department or extension number are sufficient.

Don't eat or drink on the phone!

'Susan Madeley speaking'
'Accounts department'
'2196'

Helpful tips

✔ Always have a pen or pencil and paper to hand.
✔ Answer promptly.
✔ *Never* eat or drink whilst speaking on the phone.

If the caller wants to speak to someone who is available

a find out the caller's name
b ask them to 'hold the line please' *never* 'hang on'
c tell the person requested they are wanted and by whom. (It is a good idea to use the secrecy button – just in case the person requested does not want to speak to the caller at that time!)

If the person requested is not available

a ask if you can be of help
b see if they would like to speak to someone else
c give a time when they could ring back or, depending upon company policy, offer to get the person requested to ring them back
d offer to take a message.

✔ Try not to keep callers waiting unnecessarily.
✔ Avoid spending too long speaking to a caller – it can be expensive and time-wasting *and* prevent other people from using the line.
✔ Take care not to give confidential information over the telephone.
✔ *Never* use slang words to callers

'You what?'
'OK'
'See you'.

(How many more slang expressions can you think of?)

✔ Try to use the caller's name during conversation.

'I'm sorry Mr Matthews, Mrs Fenton is not available this morning.'

✔ Always thank the caller for ringing when concluding a call.

Occasionally you will need to deal with callers who have dialled the wrong number or who have been put through to the wrong extension. Don't become impatient. Try to offer help by
- repeating your telephone number so that the caller may check whether they have misdialled
- transferring the caller to the correct extension
- returning the caller to the switchboard to be connected to the correct extension.

Find out how to transfer calls back to your switchboard or to other extensions on your telephone system.

Write down the procedure to help you to remember what to do.

Making outgoing telephone calls

The secret of making outgoing telephone calls is ... *preparation*!

Before making a call, write down
- the full code and number of the company you are calling
- the name of the person to whom you wish to speak
- full details of what you want to say – preferably in logical order.

When you have been connected
- Ask for the person, department or extension number you want.

  'Can I speak to Martin Cooper please?'
  'Personnel section please'
  'Can I have extension 2145 please?'

- Be prepared to give your name and the name of your company.
- When your call is transferred, repeat your name and company if necessary and check that you are speaking to the person requested.
- State clearly why you are making the call.
- Tick off the points on your list as they are dealt with.
- Spell out any unusual words. Use the telephone alphabet.

A – Alfred	J – Jack	S – Samuel
B – Benjamin	K – King	T – Tommy
C – Charlie	L – London	U – Uncle
D – David	M – Mary	V – Victor
E – Edward	N – Neville	W – William
F – Frederick	O – Oliver	X – X-ray
G – George	P – Peter	Y – Yellow
H – Harry	Q – Queen	Z – Zebra
I – Isaac	R – Robert	

- Make a written note of important facts.
- Conclude the call by thanking the person for their help.

Practise finding telephone numbers quickly.

You will need a copy of your local telephone directory.

Look up the telephone numbers for the following organisations and services in your area. Write them down to compare with the other members of your group. See who is the first to finish.

1 Town Hall
2 Your local hospital (with Casualty Dept)
3 Nearest international airport
4 British Rail Timetable Enquiries
5 Job Centre
6 Gas Board (to report a gas escape in your area)
7 Social Security Office
8 AA 24-Hour Breakdown Service

Can you find these international codes from your local directory?

9 Dublin, Southern Ireland
10 Tenerife
11 Rome
12 Munich

Did you find all these numbers and codes? Your geographical knowledge may help with the last three!

Confirming telephone arrangements

To avoid misunderstandings or appointments being forgotten, a telephone call is often followed by some form of written confirmation eg

- a job appointment confirmed by letter
- an order for goods confirmed by an official order form
- meetings confirmed by either letter or memo
- accommodation bookings confirmed by letter.

Answering machines

Telephone answering machines enable callers to leave messages when the telephone is not manned (eg lunch times or outside normal working hours).

A tape with a pre-recorded message invites callers to leave a message after a special tone is heard. Later the tape is rewound and the messages played back. The same tape is generally re-used.

Tips for leaving messages
✔ Begin to speak only *after* the special tone.
✔ Announce clearly who you are (and the name of your company).
✔ State who the message is for.
✔ Spell out any unusual words eg names, addresses.
✔ Make the message fairly brief or the tape will run out.
✔ Ring off.

Practise leaving the following messages on an answering machine. (You could use an ordinary tape recorder with a blank tape.)

Assume you work for the Textile Manufacturing Company who are suppliers of soft furnishings to the hotel and restaurant business. Their telephone number is 374653.

Your supervisor, Mrs Meredith, has asked you to telephone the following businesses. She has warned you that most of them will be busy at lunch time and will probably have their answering machines switched on.

Make notes beforehand to ensure that your messages are accurate and clearly delivered.

Message 1 – Kingfisher Restaurant
Tell Mr Saunders that the workshop has finished making the drapes for the two bay windows in the lounge. Two fitters could come over and fix the drapes on Friday of next week. (Make sure you give the correct date.) Ask Mr Saunders to telephone Mrs Meredith as soon as possible to let her know whether morning or afternoon would be most suitable. Be sure to leave our company telephone number.

Message 2 – Planet Hotel
Thank the Manager for his telephone enquiry. Inform him that we can renew linings to existing curtains. Tell him our estimator will be in the area next Monday (give the date). If he would like the estimator to call, ask him to telephone Mrs Meredith and we can arrange a convenient time. Give him our telephone number.

Mention that we are running a special promotion for the next two weeks. We are offering a 25 per cent discount on all dry-cleaning. Our estimator can supply details.

Message 3 – Rooftop Bar
Ask Mrs Templeton to telephone our estimator, John Prescott, to confirm which of the two designs she has chosen for the seating in the restaurant. Remind her that 'Magnolia' is the design with the blue background and 'Petunia' is the multi-floral design. Tell her that the fitters will be able to complete the refurbishment of the restaurant by the end of this month.

Telephone reference books
Your most valuable reference book should be the one compiled by you! A notebook with the telephone numbers of people who you call regularly is easy to refer to.

Other directories should include:
- local phone book
- local *Yellow Pages*
- directories for areas called regularly
  (eg London, Manchester, Birmingham)
- Thomson's local
- an alphabetical list of the names of people working in your company with their extension numbers.

Telephone services

100	For operator help in making a UK call, 24 hours a day
150 personal customers **152 business customers**	For information on BT products, services, phone book entries or other enquiries
151 personal customers **154 business customers**	To report a fault, 24 hours a day
153	To obtain an international number, 24 hours a day (However, most international calls can be made direct using IDD service.)
155	For operator help in making an international call
192	For directory enquiries (You will be asked for the name and town. There is a charge for this service.)
8081	Accurist timeline (Used to be known as speaking clock.)
Freefone 0800	No charge for using this service. (All freefone numbers are prefixed 0800. Companies offer this service to encourage and promote business.)

Telephone faults

- Sometimes a bad connection can result in a crossed line, faint volume or line interference. It is better to ring off and try again rather than persevere.
- Whenever a particular number is difficult to obtain, ask the operator (dial 100) to check the line. It is possible that the receiver has not been correctly replaced.
- Report faulty equipment as soon as possible, rather than hope the fault will correct itself.
- BT now prides itself on dealing with most faults on private lines within one working day and on business lines, within five hours!
- To report a fault, private customers should dial 151, business customers 154.

Telephone charge rates

It is important to be aware of the different **call rates** which relate to different times of the day and the day of the week.

- **peak rate**   9 am – 1 pm   Monday to Friday
- **standard rate**   8 am – 9 am
1 pm – 6 pm } Monday to Friday
- **cheap rate**   6 pm – 8 am   Monday to Friday
and   6 pm Friday – 8 am Monday   (weekend)

Charges vary depending on the distance being called. Distances are given in your local telephone directory under the section on 'Charging information'. BT also issue **charge booklets** for reference.

Remember

Telephone charges depend on

- the **call rate** (peak, standard or cheap)
- the **distance** being called (local, national or international)
- the **duration** of the call (calculated in units).

For obvious reasons, many business telephone systems bar employees from making international connections.

An itemised print-out of calls can be requested to help keep a check on telephone costs.

Security procedures and emergencies

Bomb threat	**Don't panic!** Try to obtain as much information as possible from the caller – time, whereabouts.
Confidentiality	*Never* give confidential information over the telephone. You may be overheard by someone listening in on an extension.
Emergencies	Dial 999 for police, fire or ambulance.

Under Emergencies:
- State which service is wanted.
- Give clear details of the emergency (including your name, address and telephone number).
- Answer any other questions clearly eg directions to the scene.

Section review

Complete the sentences below, using each of the following words once only.

TouchTone   message
answering   extensions
cheap   freefone
secrecy   reference
VDU   peak

1 To prevent callers overhearing your conversations with colleagues, you should press the _____ button.

2 Between 9 am and 1 pm, telephone calls are charged at _____ rate.

3 A large modern PABX switchboard could be linked to a ____ enabling the operator to view the system at one time.

4 _____ telephones are only available for customers connected to a modernised digital exchange.

5 Calls made at weekends are charged at _____ rate.

6 An _____ machine is ideal for those people who are not always available to answer the telephone.

7 If the person requested by the caller is unavailable, you should offer to take a _____.

8 On a multiline system, up to 80 _____ can be accommodated.

9 A selection of _____ books should always be kept near the telephone.

10 _____ numbers begin with 0800.

WORDSEARCH

Look at the grid shown below and find the following words.

FAULTS

STANDARD

EMERGENCY

CHARGES

CHEAP

OPERATOR

DIRECTORY

INTERNAL

SECURITY

YELLOW PAGES

R	B	O	P	E	R	A	T	O	R	S
D	I	R	E	C	T	O	R	Y	E	Y
J	N	S	G	H	J	I	Y	G	E	C
C	T	R	H	E	J	K	A	Y	S	N
H	E	S	W	A	Z	P	X	N	T	E
A	R	D	G	P	W	F	H	G	A	G
R	N	G	T	O	E	A	W	S	N	R
G	A	L	L	P	I	U	T	E	D	E
E	L	L	A	S	X	L	C	Q	A	M
S	E	C	U	R	I	T	Y	Y	R	E
Y	S	E	Q	S	D	S	G	Y	D	T

2.2 Receive and relay oral and written messages

This section covers

- rules for taking messages
- telephone messages
- effective questioning
- passing on information.

Telephone callers and face-to-face callers will often ask you to pass a **message** on to someone who is not immediately available.

It is important therefore to have the following to hand:
- pen or pencil
- scrap paper for jotting down notes
- message pad on which to write out the messages neatly.

There is no excuse for keeping callers waiting with 'Just let me get a pen,' or 'Wait whilst I find some paper.'

Rules for taking messages

- Ask for the caller's name and company at the beginning of the conversation. You will then be able to use their name during your conversation.
- Ask who the message is for – the caller is not always sure who is dealing with the matter.
- Listen to the message carefully, jotting down important points eg figures, names, times, dates.
- Do not attempt to write down *everything* the caller says – it is not necessary!
- Ask for clarification on days – eg 'next Wednesday' – find out the exact date.
- Ask for the telephone and extension number of the caller if they want a return call.
- Check important facts by repeating times, dates, names and figures to the caller.
- Use the telephone alphabet to clarify similar sounding names eg Mr **P**arker or Mr **B**arker.
- Write out the message neatly as soon as the caller has left or rung off. It can be forgotten if left!
- Write your message in simple, sentence form. Brief notes are often not clear eg 'Will ring'. 'Confirm'.
- Decide whether the message is urgent and therefore needs to be passed on immediately.

Read through these messages.

What's wrong with them?

MEMO ☎

From: The Manager - West End Garage
To: Mr Lincoln

Message: The figures which you wanted are as follows: Van Service £90, Seat Covers £20 - making a total of £120. Can you let him have a cheque asap?

Tel no - 374988
Ext no - 2169
Date: 11 March 199—
Message received by: Andrea at 2.30 pm

MESSAGE

For Joan Appleton
From Peter Green
Company Nat West
Date 12 March 199—
Time 9 am
Urgent/non-urgent

Arrive 12 noon. Take taxi. Will bring accounts. Ring.

Tel: 0293 482173 × 3174

Taken by Michael

MESSAGE FOR: Peter Stancliffe **FROM:** Sheila Gardner
of Jones and Clayton
DATE: 10 March 199
TIME:

TELEPHONE CODE 0405 NUMBER 632198 EXT — TAKEN BY: Louise

MESSAGE
Can you please ring Sheila Gardner within the next hour?

TELEPHONED ✓	PLEASE RING BACK ✓	RETURNED YOUR CALL ☐
WILL RING BACK ☐	WOULD LIKE TO SEE YOU ☐	URGENT ✓

MEMO ☎

From: Mrs Lucas
To: Mr Lincoln

Message: Mrs Lucas wants you to phone her about the estimate which you gave her for the kitchen. She will be at her daughter's house for the rest of the day. Can you ring her there?

Date: 8 March 199—
Message received by: Andrea at 10.40 am

MEMO ☎

From: Jade Fenton - PKT Ltd
To: Joan Appleton

Message: Can you book overnight accommodation (B+B only) for the 4 reps from London for the night of 27 March? The reps' names are Jeremy Walton, Claire Jenkins and Simon Scott.

Tel no - 321758
Ext no - 1947
Date: 9 March 199—
Message received by: Andrea at 11 am

MESSAGE

For Mr Parkinson
From Mr Sinclair
Company Head Office
Date 7 March 199—
Time 3.15 pm
Urgent/non-urgent

The monthly meeting for next month has had to be changed. It will now be on Thursday.

Taken by Louise

Telephone messages

There are many different types of message pad available such as the following: a pad of blank notes with adhesive strip on reverse, enabling them to be stuck down to any surface; a pad of printed telephone message sheets; a book of tear-out message sheets with NCR duplicate copy to be kept for reference; scrap paper kept by the phone! Cheap but adequate.

Whichever type of message sheet is used, *always* include
- name (and company) of caller
- telephone and extension number
- date and time of call
- details of the message
- the name of the person who has taken the message.

Effective questioning

In order to pass on a complete message, you will often have to ask the caller for more information.

Questions should be asked in a courteous manner and not 'fired' at the caller.

'Who for?'
'How much?'
'What time?'

Abrupt questions such as these can give a bad impression.

It can be helpful to the person receiving the message if you can give some indication as to why the caller is telephoning.

Compare these two messages.

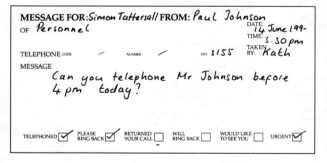
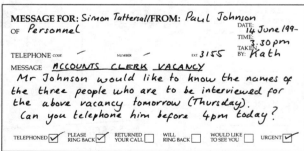

If Mr Tattersall is given the message on the right, he can make sure he has the information requested to hand *before* he returns Mr Johnson's call.

Sometimes callers automatically ask for a person in a senior position because they believe that person is dealing with the matter. By effective questioning, you may discover that the message can easily be dealt with by a secretary, an assistant or even yourself!

Passing on information

- Urgent messages must always be passed on immediately. If the person who the message is for will not be returning for some time, it is advisable to see if someone else can deal with the message.

- Occasionally, it can be helpful to give some information verbally with your message.

  'Miss Lewis was extremely upset.'

- Always write down messages. Never rely on remembering to tell the person – you will most likely forget!

Section review

Fill in the missing letters, then write the completed words in your folder to help you remember them.

1 As well as the telephone number, it is advisable to obtain the caller's e___ns__n number so that the call can be returned quickly.

2 If you need to clarify the spelling of a name, use the telephone a_ph_b__.

3 When making appointments, if is better to obtain the d__ and date to prevent confusion.

4 To obtain sufficient information to pass on a message, you often need to q__s___n the caller.

5 If a message is u_g__t, it should be passed on immediately.

6 When answering the telephone, you should always have a __n or __nc_l to hand.

7 As well as a written message, it is useful to pass on v__b_l information.

8 All messages should be written out clearly and n__tl_.

9 A friendly impression is created if you use the caller's n___ occasionally during a telephone conversation.

10 As well as the date, you should always record the t___ when a message is received.

2.3 Supply information for a specific purpose

This section covers

- information sources
- how to use reference books
- presentation methods
- deadlines and targets.

? 'Can you find me the phone number for Heathrow Airport?'
? 'Where can I find the name of a magician for my daughter's birthday party next week?'
? 'Do not type the penultimate paragraph.' What does penultimate mean?
? 'How far is it by road from Cardiff to Liverpool?'
? 'Which motorway will I need to use when travelling from Bristol to Exeter?'

Do you know where to look for the above information?

- Airport telephone numbers are listed at the beginning of all local telephone directories.
- A magician would be listed under 'entertainers' in *Yellow Pages*.
- The meaning of penultimate can be found in a dictionary.
- Mileage distance charts are given in books such as the AA handbook, diaries and road map books.
- Motorways are shown on most UK road maps.

Information sources

Where do you look for information?

- **People who you work with** have a wealth of knowledge about the company, its products and working procedures – acquired from years of experience.
- **Organisations to contact**
  - Citizen's Advice Bureau (CAB)
  - Chamber of Commerce
  - Town Hall
  - County Council
  - Department of Social Security
  - Inland Revenue
  - Insurance brokers
  - British Rail
  - AA and RAC
  - Travel agents
  - Banks
- **Royal Mail**
  - **Post Office Counters Ltd** for leaflets on postage services and current postage rates, one-year passports and motor vehicle taxation.
  - **Letter delivery offices** for enquiries regarding deliveries of letters.
  - **Parcelforce** for all types of parcel delivery services.
- **British Telecom** for details of all telecommunication services.
- **Local Reference Library** – to research information from reference books, periodicals and computer databases. Back issues of newspapers are often kept on microfiche. (Photocopying facilities are usually available for a small charge.)
- **Viewdata, Prestel** – over 250 000 pages of information can be viewed on computer screen. Reservations can be made via the keyboard.
- **Teletext**
  - Ceefax (BBC) } Pages of information can be viewed at home
  - Oracle (IBA) } on the television screen.

- **Newspapers** (local and national)
  As well as current news articles, daily temperatures, currency exchange rates and share values are given.
- **Magazines**
  Specialist trade publications
  Consumer magazines such as *Which?*
- **Telecommunications directories**
  Telephone
  Yellow Pages
  Telex
  Fax
- **Reference books**
  - **Dictionary** for spellings, meanings and pronunciation of words. Also includes the meanings of commonly-used abbreviations.
  - **Thesaurus** gives alternative meanings of words
    Pear's Cyclopaedia for information on a variety of topics – published annually
  - ***Whitaker's Almanack*** a general reference book – published annually
  - **Atlas** for maps and other information
  - **Road maps, A-Z street guides** useful for people who travel a lot
  - ***Fowler's Modern English Usage*** to check points of grammar
  - ***Titles and Forms of Address*** by Black gives the correct way to address a titled person
  - ***Who's Who*** published annually and gives brief details of famous people. Other publications include *Who Was Who* and *International Who's Who*
  - **AA and RAC handbooks** for details of hotels, UK road maps, main town street maps and other types of motorist information

Ask your tutor to let you look at a business desk diary for the current year.

Make a list of all the different types of information contained in the pages at the front.

Compare your list with those of others in your group who have looked at different diaries. Did you realise that all this information is so easy to find?

How to use reference books
- Check that the reference book which you are using is up to date.
- Make sure you know how to find information quickly from books. Rather than just flicking through the pages, refer to the contents page listed at the beginning.
- If you still can't find what you are looking for, check the index or glossary which is listed in alphabetical order at the end of the book.
- If you can't find the topic you are looking for, it could possibly be listed under another word
  Prestel would be found under **V**iewdata systems
  Tally rolls under **A**dd listing rolls
- When using several reference books, place strips of card between the pages you want to use. It saves time if you have to keep turning back to the same pages.

Where would you look for the following information?

1 A four-star hotel in Blackpool (*two* sources)

2 Today's currency exchange rate for the French franc (*three* sources)

3 Flight availability information to Portugal (*two* sources)

4 Biographical details of a well-known MP

5 The meaning of the word 'ambiguous'

6 The distance between two UK towns (*three* sources)

7 Details of tonight's BBC TV programmes (*three* sources)

8 Yesterday's temperature in Majorca (*two* sources)

9 The cost of a provisional driving licence

10 The last guaranteed postal date for posting Christmas parcels to Australia

Presentation methods

When you have found the information, pass it on quickly to the person who requested it.

You can do this in several ways.

Oral response

Avoid passing on information verbally unless

- it is wanted immediately
- it is short and uncomplicated
- the person can write it down immediately.

Figures, times and amounts of money should always be passed on in writing to avoid confusion.

Written form

Information can be passed on by a

- note
- memo
- letter.

(See section 2.4, page **35** for composition of business correspondence.)

Graph

Some information is better displayed in graph form.

- Line graphs
- Histograms
- Bar charts
- Pie charts

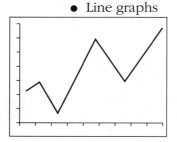 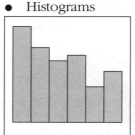 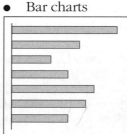 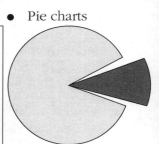

List

Information presented in a list or in table form is clear and easy to follow.

CLIENT TELEPHONE NUMBERS

R.J. SALISBURY & CO	0764 245663
MASONS TELEVISION REPAIR	0764 278754
THAXTED INSURANCE PURVEYORS	0783 963842
SPIEGELERS OFFICE SUPPLIES	0764 193334
CROMWELL'S AND SONS BUTCHERS	0764 632054
CHERRYTREE OAP HOME	0597 548
BIXLER'S BIKES	0764 654198

COMPANY HOLIDAY ROTA

JAMES	ROGER	ELAIN	JACKIE	SAM
30-5 JANUARY	13-17 JANUARY	27-30 JANUARY	1-5 JANUARY	28-4 APRIL
5-22 JUNE	4-8 MAY	25-29 JUNE	8-18 MARCH	4-9 MAY
2-5 OCTOBER	22-26 JULY	3-8 OCTOBER	2-5 AUGUST	6-10 JULY
9-11 NOVEMBER	2 OCTOBER	1-3 NOVEMBER	23-24 SEPTEMBER	7-11 SEPTEMBER
	12-13 OCTOBER	12-19 NOVEMBER	9-11 NOVEMBER	7-11 DECEMBER
	9-11 NOVEMBER			

Deadlines and targets

When you are asked to find out information
- Try to deal with the request immediately.
- Ask for more details if you are having difficulty finding the information.
- Let the person requesting the information know if there will be a delay eg telephone line engaged.
- Try not to get side-tracked by doing another job, or by chatting!
- As soon as you have obtained the information, pass it on immediately in the most suitable form.

'I'll get that information Mrs Pearson wants urgently – as soon as I've put the kettle on and told you about my new boyfriend!'

Section review

Complete the sentences below, using each of the following words, once only.

Viewdata   deadline
colleagues   graph
directory   newspapers
index   dictionary
microfiche   oral

1 A _____ gives the pronunciation of words as well as the meaning.

2 Fax, telex and telephone numbers can all be found in the appropriate _____.

3 Prestel is a _____ system which offers over 250 000 different pages of information.

4 Past issues of newspapers in a reference library are stored on _____.

5 A lot of valuable information can be obtained just by asking _____.

6 Suitable methods of presenting information can include note, memo, letter or _____ response.

7 When using a reference book, look for the topic in either the contents page or the _____.

8 Try to keep to the required _____ when supplying information to senior colleagues.

9 As well as news articles, _____ contain daily temperatures, currency exchange rates and share prices.

10 Visual information is often displayed in _____ form.

Find out the following information from the most appropriate source

1 The cost of a one-year single passport

2 The telephone code number for inner London

3 The name of the stretch of sea separating the Isle of Wight from the UK mainland

4 What the abbreviation MEP stands for

5 Yesterday's temperature in Miami

6 The price of a weekday edition of *The Times* newspaper

7 The capital of Malta

8 The cost of a road fund licence for a private vehicle for one year

9 The maiden name of Baroness Margaret Thatcher

10 What the abbreviation CV stands for

2.4 Draft routine business communications

This section covers

- using correct grammar
- improving spelling
- punctuation
- extending vocabulary
- letters
- memos.

Many people today are not confident about writing letters and memos. You needn't be one of them. Pay attention to improving your basic **writing skills**.

Using correct grammar

You might wonder why it is important to use correct grammar. It might not be important when you are talking to your friends, but when you are writing letters for your company it is.

Letters must be clear and understandable. Every letter you send is an ambassador for the company you work for. To make sure each letter is right it is helpful to know some basic grammar, so you can check what you write is correct.

Nouns and verbs

A **noun** can be a person, place or thing.

eg David, girl, Brighton, kitchen, book, purse

A **verb** is a doing word which illustrates an action.
To find out whether a word is a verb, see if it makes sense with the word 'to' in front of it.

eg to read   to ask
to write   to employ

A sentence must contain at least a **noun** (subject) and a **verb** (action). If the action is being done to someone or something, that thing is the **object** of the sentence, and is also a noun or a pronoun.

eg subject   verb
Terry shouted.
subject   verb   object
The clerk posted the letter.

Sentences start with a capital letter and end with a full stop.

Incomplete sentences

Make sure you write complete sentences, *not*

With regard to your letter.
Despite the interest shown.
Because of the cost involved.

These are not complete sentences. Beware! Don't be someone who starts letters 'Dear Saroj, With regard to your letter of 25 September.' *Try*, 'Dear Saroj, Thank you for your letter of 25 September.' This second example has the verb 'thank'.

Singular and plural

Remember:

singular	plural
I am	We are
John is	Tom and Jill are
She was	They were
I was	We were

Collective nouns can cause problems.

eg group   government   class   team

The government *is* to be recalled.
A list of books *has* been given to the librarian.
A variety of papers *is* stored in the cabinet.

Only *one* Government, so a singular verb.
List is the subject of the second sentence. There's only one list even if there are many books on it, so a singular verb.

Rewrite the following sentences correctly by changing the word in italics.

1   The children forgot to tell their mother where they *was* going

2   Adults are *learnt* new skills to help them find work.

3   The hotel *are* offering special discounts to guests staying the night.

4   We haven't been *nowhere* for our holidays this year.

5   Which of the twins is the *tallest*?

6   Mary and June *is* going to be late for college.

Check your answers with the key.

If you have got a sentence wrong, check the mistake with your tutor.

Lots of people muddle 'learn' and 'teach/taught'. Remember, people *learn* things but a teacher must *teach* them. If you're not sure which to use, always check in your dictionary.

Don't use double negatives – *not* with *nothing, no-one, nowhere*, etc. The effect is to cancel the negative. If 'I've not got nothing' then maybe I have something! Not the message I want to give.

Big, bigger, biggest; good, better, best. If you are comparing only two things (and twins come in twos) then you need only the first two adjectives: big and bigger; or tall and taller etc. If you have more than two things to compare then you need to use an adjective ending in – est.
     eg Chris types fastest.
       Who is the fairest if them all?

In the final sentence the subject is plural – Mary *and* Jane: *they are* both going to be late for college.

Improving spelling

Certain words which are used regularly in business correspondence are unfortunately often misspelt. It is worth taking the effort to learn troublesome words. (In the long run it will save you time because you won't need to look them up in a dictionary each time you write or type them.)

Look at the following group of words. Make sure you can spell each word correctly. Copy down those which you are unsure of.

Afterwards cover each group and ask your tutor to dictate them to you so that you can write them down.

Check carefully that you have spelt each one correctly.

Group 1 – adding 'ly'

late	lately	comparative	comparatively
sincere	sincerely	approximate	approximately
unfortunate	unfortunately	separate	separately
rare	rarely	accurate	accurately
complete	completely	extreme	extremely

Remember – just add 'ly' to the original word.

Group 2 – past tenses

		Exceptions
omit	omitted	benefited
refer	referred	answered
permit	permitted	lowered
occur	occurred	
transfer	transferred	
cancel	cancelled	
submit	submitted	
enrol	enrolled	
commit	committed	
incur	incurred	
initial	initialled	

Note – in this group of words, the consonant at the end of the original word has been doubled.

Group 3 – silent letters

Some words contain letters which are not sounded

plumber	scissors
column	government
prompt	length
chaos	schedule (depending on pronunciation)
ghost	psychology
depot	environment

Group 4 – in words which are pronounced **ee** remember **i** before **e** except after **c**.

	After 'c'	Exceptions
believe	receive	seize
thief	receipt	
achieve	ceiling	
tier	deceive	
reprieve	conceive	
grievance		
hygiene		
wield		
cashier		

Group 5 – 'double trouble'

accommodation	assessment
committee	success
commission	woollen
address	occurrence
embarrass	

Group 6 – extra care needed with these words

maintenance	February	definite
colleagues	competent	surprise
exercise	guarantee	liaison
catalogue	opportunity	separate
definite	recommend	business
necessary	signature	secretary
until	whether	procedure

Learn a group a week, and you'll soon master these difficult words.

Remember

You should always have a dictionary handy – *if in doubt, check it out.*

Take extra care when using similar sounding words (**homonyms**). See how easy it is to choose the wrong spelling.

- I have been to there house many times. *their*
- The girl as been late for work twice this week. *has*
- The company will have to bare the cost of the accident. *bear*
- The new dress was far to small. *too*
- Come to are house for supper. *our*

Complete the following sentences selecting the correctly spelt word.

1 WERE   WHERE   WEAR
a   I prefer to _____ a uniform for work.
b   The children _____ late for the party.
c   Let me know _____ the box has been hidden.

2 THERE   THEIR
a   We are hoping _____ will be a cancellation.
b   It has been said that dogs sometimes resemble _____owners.

3 TO   TOO   TWO
a   The restaurant had prepared _____ many meals.
b   Can you find _____ more books for me to borrow?
c   They agreed _____ delay the start of the game.

4 AS   HAS
a   Joanne _____ seen a jacket which will match her new skirt.
b   You should always check calculations _____ it is easy to make a mistake.

5 FARE   FAIR
a   The _____ from Bristol to London has recently been increased.
b   It is not _____ when people refuse to wait their turn.

6 OF   OFF
a   They were given instructions to turn ____ the electricity.
b   Try to arrive at a new job with plenty ____ time to spare.

7 NO   KNOW
a   Can you let your supervisor _____ whether you are able to work on Saturday?
b   There will be _____ more postal deliveries today.

8 CHECK   CHEQUE
a   I made out a _____ to pay the electricity account.
b   It is a good idea to use a calculator to _____ figures.

Punctuation
CAPITAL LETTERS

- Sentences must begin with a **capital letter** and end with a **full stop**. Occasionally, a **question mark** or **exclamation mark** can take the place of a full stop.

  How did you enjoy the film?
  Beware of the dog!

- **Proper nouns** must begin with a **capital letter**.

  James and Catherine went to Rome for their holidays.
  We are going to Ramsey in the Isle of Man.
  I have an interview with the Personnel Manager, Ian Kennedy.
  Next year, Easter falls in April.

- The word **I** is *always* written with a **capital letter**, whether used at the *beginning* or in the *middle* of a sentence.

  I often wish that I had paid more attention at school.

Hyphens –

A hyphen is used

- to connect two 'describing' words

  well-mannered   *three-sided*   *cost-effective*

- to split a word at the end of a line.

  We have arranged for the entertain-
  ment after the presentation of the prizes.

Dashes –

A dash is used to give a pause within a sentence.

  A receptionist should be courteous to all callers –
  they could be future customers.

Semi-colons ;

A semi-colon can be used to separate two clauses in a sentence.

  The sky was black; it would soon begin to rain.

Colons :

A colon is used before introducing a list.

  The girl had many interests: netball, swimming, roller-skating and tennis.

Apostrophe '

1 An apostrophe is used to show ownership

- **before** the 's', to indicate *one* owner

  my dog's ball   *Simon's coat*

- **after** the 's', to indicate *more than one* owner.

  girls' toilets   *boys' classroom*

When referring to units of time

- **before** the 's', if *singular*

  one hour's drive   *one year's pay*

- **after** the 's', if *plural*

  four days' wages   *seven weeks' time*

- **ordinary plural** words *do not* need an apostrophe.

  hotels   *letters*   *caravans*   *books*

Exception: **It's** always means *it is.*

  It's time to go.

Do *not* use the apostrophe for

  The bird was in its cage.

2 An apostrophe shows that a letter or letters are missing from a word

I have … I've	who have … who've
you will … you'll	you have … you've
there is … there's	is not … isn't
cannot … can't	does not … doesn't
have not … haven't	you are … you're
who would … who'd	I would … I'd
we are … we're	who is … who's
of the clock … o'clock	*and of course*, it is … it's

Rewrite the following sentences inserting apostrophes where appropriate.

- Isnt the house cold?
- I hope youll return Johns letter.
- Theres a problem with Jacks car.
- Well arrive at the managers office at 9oclock.
- We cant decide if its going to be a problem.

Extending vocabulary

When people say 'I can't write letters' what they really mean is 'I can never think of the correct words to use.'

They have a **limited vocabulary**!

Vocabulary can be extended by
- reading – books, newspapers or magazines
- listening to news programmes on TV or radio
- doing wordsearch puzzles and crosswords
- asking people to explain the meaning of an unfamiliar word
- checking the meaning of new words in a dictionary.

Why not keep a notebook with a separate page for each letter of the alphabet? Each week, make a point of writing down 10 new words. After one year, you will know the meaning of 500 new words and – hopefully – be able to spell each one correctly! Just think – after five years …

Read through the sentences below. Notice the words written in italics. Check their meaning in a dictionary and find an alternative word or words which mean the same.

1 The clerk said she would give the customer a *facsimile* copy.

2 The teacher agreed that the question was *ambiguous*.

3 The newspaper published the letter knowing it would *provoke* much response.

4 A number of people were invited to *participate*.

5 The police could not find any evidence to *substantiate* the claim.

Letters

In business, letters are used to request and pass on information between firms and individuals.

These could include
- letters of enquiry
- letters giving information
- letters confirming appointments
- letters of complaint
- letters to job applicants
- letters of reminder
- circular letters
- form letters.

To create a good impression, a business letter should
- be correctly set out
- be neatly typed with no errors or messy corrections
- be courteous and polite – not abrupt or nasty
- not have any spelling, punctuation or grammatical errors.

Most business letters today are set out in fully-blocked style with open punctuation. Look at the example below.

Interior Design Company

Lakeland House, Orpington Place, Oxford OX2 3PZ TEL: 0865-473527 FAX: 0865-246678

Our ref NE/GHT
Your ref 234/RT

14 April 199

Mr Paul Hastings
Texline Products plc
41 Highbury Gardens
OXFORD
OX2 9TX

Dear Mr Hastings

REFURBISHMENT OF RECEPTION AREA

Thank you for your letter of 10 April returning fabric samples. I note your comments with regard to styles and enclose one of our design brochures for you to look at.

I have arranged for work to commence on Monday, 21 April next. It would assist our fitters if the whole of the reception area could be cleared of furniture before they arrive. The work should take three days to complete so the area should be useable by Thursday, 24 April.

If you require any further information about the work, please do not hesitate to contact me.

Yours sincerely
INTERIOR DESIGN COMPANY

N Edwards

Nigel Edwards
Manager

Points to remember

✓ Use a heading, if necessary – it can save a long explanation of what the letter is about.

```
VACANCY FOR ACCOUNTS CLERK
Patent No 73456
```

✓ Although punctuation is omitted from the date, name and address of the addressee, full stops and commas should be used in the body of the letter to assist the reader.

✓ An opening paragraph sets the scene.

We thank you for your letter...
As arranged at our meeting yesterday...

Never

I am writing this letter to tell you...
With reference to your letter of...

✓ The middle paragraph(s) should cover the reasons for writing the letter eg to give information, to offer an explanation, to request more detail.

✓ The last paragraph should conclude the letter in a friendly manner.

If you require any further information, please...
We look forward to hearing from you...

✓ The salutation and complimentary close should match.

Dear Sir (Madam)   use   *Yours faithfully*
Dear Mr Kinder   use   *Yours sincerely*

✓ Do not ramble on trying to make the letter longer than necessary. Some letters only need to be short!

You work for Peter Anderson, the Valuations Director of Shireburn Homes Ltd. He has asked you to prepare three letters for him to sign on his return to the office later. His written instructions for the letters are set out below.

Letter 1

Write to Mrs Susan Parkinson of The Evergreens, Valley Road, Churchtown, CH5 7RD. I spoke to her by telephone yesterday and arranged to call at her house on Friday of next week at 2.30 pm. Can you confirm this appointment?

Ask her to collect her house deeds from her bank so that I can check who owns the plot of land at the rear of her house.

Letter 2

Write to Tony Parks of Jubilee Garage, Singleton Road, Churchtown CH1 4FG. Thank him for his letter dated yesterday.

Tell him I have discussed the question of car leasing with my fellow directors and would like more information from him. Ask him to send some quotations for me to look at.

In the meantime, ask him to collect the Escort van next Thursday for a six-monthly service.

Tone

A business letter is usually written more formally than a letter to a friend. Compare the differences in tone in the following excerpts.

Business letter	Letter to a friend
If you require further information do not hesitate to telephone me	Give me a ring
Thank you for your letter of yesterday	How nice to hear from you
An early reply will be appreciated	Drop me a line early next week
I suggest that we meet to discuss the matter	Let's meet so we can catch up on what's happened

Letters to friends are more chatty and often written in the same tone we would use if we were speaking to that person.

It is important when you are sending out letters for your company that you use a business-like tone.

Memos

- **Memo** is the abbreviated form for the word **memorandum**. The plural of memorandum is memoranda (not memorandums).
- A memo is used when writing to people who work in your own organisation.
- Memos do not need to show the recipient's address because they are usually going to someone in your own building.
- They should be kept short and to the point.
- If the memo is to contain a considerable amount of information, divide this into numbered points for clarity.
- A salutation and complimentary close are also unnecessary, although the sender sometimes initials the memo at the end.
- Memos dealing with a confidential matter should be marked 'Confidential'. They should be put in a sealed envelope, similarly marked.

Here are two examples of memo layout.

M E M O R A N D U M

From   Louise Nelson   Ref   LN/

To   Charles Kay   Date   24 January 199-

MARKETING MEETING

The date for next month's marketing meeting has had to be changed because Mr Parker will be in Germany on that date.

The meeting has been rescheduled for 27 February at 10 am in the Board Room.

LN

MEMORANDUM

To   Jane Fairfax

From   Mike Newton

Date   12 January 199-

Ref   MN/ASD

Holiday Rota

I attach the holiday rota list for this year.

Will you please make sure that everyone in your department enters the dates when they would like to take their holidays.

Can I remind you that where more than three people want to take their holidays at the same time, those in the most senior positions have first choice.

MN

Enc

Your boss, Jeremy Lucas, has asked you to book a single room with private facilities for Thursday of next week (one night – bed and breakfast only) at the Carlton Hotel, Brighton. You have made the reservation by telephone and sent them a letter confirming the booking.

Write a **memo** to your boss confirming what you have done.

Section review

Complete the missing letters, then write the words in your folder to help you remember them.

1   A _yph_n is used to connect two words.

2   If you are unsure about the spelling of a word, check with a _ _ ct_ _ n_ry.

3   A _ _ _ o is a written communication to someone in your own organisation.

4   Yours faithfully is a type of c_ _pl_m_ _t_ry close.

5   The _p_st_ _ _h_ is a punctuation sign used to show ownership.

6   Reading a newspaper regularly will help to extend your _ _c_b_l_ _y.

7   Memos should, if possible, be kept _ _ _rt.

8   A c_ _ _n is used before introducing a list.

9   Business letters are generally set out in full-blocked s_y_ _.

10 All written communications should be checked carefully for errors in _p_ll_ _g.

WORDSEARCH

Look at the grid shown below and find the following words.

GRAMMAR

LAYOUT

SALUTATION

CONFIRMATION

LETTER

SPELLING

DASH

ENQUIRY

SENTENCE

PUNCTUATION

C	R	W	S	P	E	L	L	I	N	G	D
S	O	D	F	V	X	X	F	Y	R	E	P
A	E	N	Q	U	I	R	Y	C	S	H	U
Q	L	V	F	B	R	Y	H	P	W	S	N
H	A	E	B	I	W	P	V	R	K	A	C
D	Y	C	B	W	R	K	Y	E	W	D	T
B	O	N	G	R	A	M	M	A	R	W	U
P	U	E	D	F	H	J	A	D	W	U	A
V	T	T	J	H	L	E	T	T	E	R	T
S	X	N	K	L	Q	S	T	P	I	W	I
D	B	E	K	R	E	T	Y	H	J	O	O
S	W	S	A	L	U	T	A	T	I	O	N

3 Data processing

3.1 Produce alpha/numerical information in typewritten form

This section covers

- keyboard equipment
- technique and posture
- care and maintenance of equipment
- correction of errors
- styles of layout
- reference aids
- saving and printing data.

If you have the opportunity of learning to type, it is well worth the time and effort.

Keyboarding accounts for a large proportion of clerical jobs today, from copy typist to secretary and sales assistant to stock control clerk.

Can you think of *six* different types of job which involve using a keyboard during some part of the day?

Keyboard equipment

Manual typewriter
Not used a lot these days! Plenty of effort is needed to strike the keys – and return the carriage.

Electric typewriter
A power supply helps make pressing the keys and using repeat keys far easier.

Electronic typewriter
A reduction in price during the last few years has enabled even the smallest of offices to replace their manuals and electrics with these multi-functional machines.

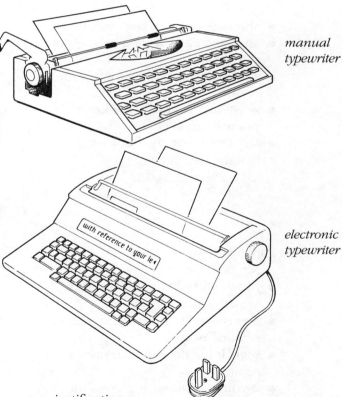

manual typewriter

electronic typewriter

Facilities include
- word wraparound
- easy correction of errors
- text emboldening
- automatic centring of words
- choice of pitch (size of type)
- justification
- paragraph indent
- drawing lines
- storage of paragraphs into memory
- small display screen.

Word processor

This has an electronic keyboard with VDU (visual display unit) with all the facilities of an electronic typewriter.

Keyed-in text can be printed out on an attached or shared printer.

Additional facilities include
- easy insertion and deletion of text
- moving and copying text
- mail merge
- spelling check
- storage of work to disk.

Technique and posture

Whichever type of keyboard is being used, ensure that
- fingers remain in contact with the home keys

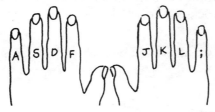

Touch typists have an advantage over those using two index fingers for the 'hunt and peck' method!

- shoulders are relaxed – not tense
- arms and elbows hang loose – not stuck out!
- adjustable back rest supports the back
- wrists are level with the keyboard – not resting on it!
- feet are flat on the floor – not dangling in mid-air.

Particularly when using VDUs, remember that
- blinds and curtains will prevent screen glare
- acoustic printer hoods can reduce printing noise
- regular breaks will help prevent eye strain
- if you need to wear glasses for close work – *wear them*!

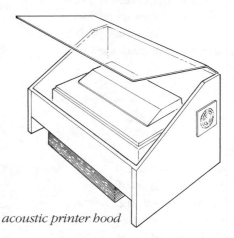

acoustic printer hood

Care and maintenance of equipment

- Keep all keyboarding equipment covered when not in use, to prevent a build up of dust.
- Clean type faces regularly with a stiff brush.
- Use keyboard brushes to remove fluff and particles from keyboard.
- Dust and wipe *outer* area of equipment with special cleaning foam – *never water*!
- Use anti-static wipes or spray to clean VDU screens.
- Make sure that all trailing cables are fastened away under desks.
- Check electric plugs regularly for loose wiring.
- Report all equipment faults immediately.
- *Never* eat or drink whilst using machinery.

Correction of errors

Manual typewriter

Use liquid paper, applied thinly and allowed to dry completely before overtyping.

Electric typewriter

A correction ribbon is usually incorporated – otherwise use liquid paper.

Electronic typewriter

All have their own correcting ribbons – avoid using liquid paper as this will spoil the daisy wheel.

Word processor

So easy – either use delete key or just type over errors!

It is easier to correct errors as soon as you see them – they can be forgotten if left until later.

Always proof-read each page carefully *before* taking the paper from your machine or storing work to disk.

Make use of the spell check facility on your word processor.

Nothing is more embarrassing than having someone point out your errors and, worse still, you having to repeat the work!

Styles of layout

Whichever method of document layout you have been taught, you will be expected to follow the style preferred by the organisation for whom you work.

Letter layout

Compare the style of layout of the three letters illustrated below.

A *Fully-blocked letter with open punctuation*

CENTRAL
ENTERPRISES
Falcon Street, Rugby, RG12 4PL.

Ref FH/TL

12 August 199_

Mrs J Scott
33 Clifton Drive
RUGBY
RG1 8GF

Dear Mrs Scott

Thank you for your letter dated 9 August enclosing the
information about your investments.

I shall be pleased if you could call to see me on Monday, 19
August at 2.30 pm when I hope to be able to give you the
remaining quotations.

Please telephone my secretary if this date is not convenient
and arrange an alternative time.

Yours sincerely

F. Hargreaves

FRANCES HARGREAVES
Finance Manager

B *Fully-blocked letter with punctuation*

Backhouse & Company
• Solicitors •
3 Hilton Road • Chester • CH2 5WD

Our ref. T5678

25th June 199_

The Manager,
Templeton & Co. Ltd.,
Station Road,
CHESTER.
CH1 3GB

Dear Sir,

James Crabtree

The above-named has applied to us for the position of despatch
clerk.

Your name has been given as a referee and we shall be grateful
if you will give us your opinion, in confidence, as to whether
he would be suitable for a position with us. We enclose a job
description for the post.

We enclose a stamped addressed envelope for your reply.

Yours faithfully,
BACKHOUSE & COMPANY,

Paul Preston

PAUL J. PRESTON.
Partner.

Enc.

W. H. LYNN & CO.
INSURANCE BROKERS
6 High Street • Carlisle • CR1 4KK

                                          22nd May 199_

Our ref. WF/KP

CONFIDENTIAL

Mr. W. T. Barnes,
67 Bridlington Road,
CARLISLE.
CR1 3GB

Dear Sir,

                    Southern & Ashworth

    The recent insurance claim which you submitted has been
forwarded to the above company. They have, however, asked for
more information to be supplied by you as to how the fire
started.

    Will you please complete the enclosed questionnaire and
return it to us as soon as possible?

                         Yours faithfully,
                         W. H. LYNN & CO.

                         S. King

                         SUSAN J. KING
                         Claims Manager.

Enc.

C *Semi-blocked letter with punctuation*

Note: A is the style favoured by most offices today.

Memo layout

Different companies have their own style of memo design.

MEMO

To   Jean Pearson   Ref   JW
From John Whiteside   Date   5 October 199_
_____

Subject - Library

M E M O R A N D U M

From   T Banks   Ref   K234
To   All Staff   Date   1 May 199_

MEMORANDUM

To   Joanne White
From Andrew Parkinson
Date 15 June 199_
Ref   AP/

Document numbering

Page numbers can go at the top or bottom of the page, in the centre, or to one side.

Whichever numbering layout is used, be consistent. Keep to the same style for each page.

Note: The first page of a document is *not* numbered.

Reference aids

When typing documents, there will be times when you need to query parts of the manuscript.

You *must*
- check with the author of the document, *or*
- use a spell check, *or*
- refer to an appropriate reference source

eg	spelling	– dictionary
	date	– diary/calendar
	post code	– post code directory.

Never guess!

Saving and printing data
Before saving work to disk, you should
- proof-read your screen very carefully for errors – if you find this difficult, print a draft copy and check this
- make sure that your document is paginated sensibly – no single words or final items of a list separated from the remaining text
- use the spell check if your spelling is not good
- make a note of the name of your document and the disk to which you are saving.

Before printing
- check that your paper is lined up straight in the printer
- take care to print out the correct document – it is a waste of time to select the wrong one!
- find out how to stop the printer quickly in the event of an emergency
- always leave the paper in the printer correctly aligned ready for the next person to use.

Section review

a The following letter and envelope comprise approximately 150 words.

Read through the letter carefully to find the spelling error in the first paragraph and then work out the date referred to in the last paragraph.

Type both letter and envelope, if possible, within 10 minutes.

Our ref   SM/AK

Today's date

Mr Mark Kingsley
43 Cherryclough Way
PRESTON
PR2 5GH

Dear Mr Kingsley

In connection with your recent booking, we are now pleased to enclose the tour operator's confirmation. Please check this carefully to ensure that the details are as shown on the booking form and if their is any discrepancy contact our office as soon as possible.

Should you or any member of your ~~family~~ *party* be forced to cancel your holiday, it is essential that we are notified immediately.

We recom*m*end that if you have *not* already done so that you take out holiday insurance immediately as it is now a booking condition of many major tour operators that all clients must be covered by insurance.

Finally, please let us have *a remittance for £893·50* the balance of your holiday by *(typist - work out the date for Friday of next week)*.

Yours sincerely

SARAH MASON
Tours Manager

Enc

Envelope required

Proof-read both documents carefully – if you make fewer than *two* errors, you are making sound progress!

b The following memo of approximately 150 words contains *five* errors.

Read through carefully to identify these errors, before typing the memo in under 10 minutes, if possible.

M E M O R A N D U M

TO   Sarah Mason, Tours Manager

FROM   Paul Henderson, Travel Manager

REF   PH/5647834

DATE   Today

CYPRUS FLIGHTS - SUMMER SCHEDULE

We have today been notified by the Tour Operator that flights to Larnaca from 30 March from Gatwick each monday have been rescheduled to ~~part~~ *depart* as follows:

FLIGHT BY472	Gatwick/Larnaca	Depart 0500 hours
FLIGHT BY473	Lanaca/Gatwick	Depart 0600 hours

Will you please notify your/*two* clients, Mr James Fairweather and Mr Gary Baker of these changes and inform them that the matter is completely out of are control?

If the resheduled times are inconvenient for your two clients, there are at present available seats on a later flight at 1400 hours but your clients must inform us of there wish to change flights before the end of next week as we are unable to hold these seats any later than then.

Proof-read your document carefully.

WORDSEARCH

Look at the grid shown below and find the following words.

TECHNIQUE

SPELLCHECK

CORRECT

LAYOUT

PRINTER

VDU

ELECTRONIC

DICTIONARY

ACOUSTIC

KEYBOARD

T	F	F	J	Z	W	I	R	M	Z	Y	K
C	S	X	P	R	I	N	T	E	R	C	C
E	J	T	K	E	Y	B	O	A	R	D	E
R	L	E	U	M	X	A	N	H	G	L	H
R	A	E	S	A	C	O	U	S	T	I	C
O	P	U	C	F	I	S	Q	D	U	M	L
C	A	Z	G	T	J	G	U	K	O	L	L
R	W	D	C	C	R	X	G	H	Y	L	E
F	D	I	A	V	G	O	C	L	A	K	P
V	D	U	Y	D	R	B	N	G	L	G	S
F	H	R	T	E	C	H	N	I	Q	U	E
S	Q	S	G	J	O	L	M	T	C	R	S

3.2 Identify and mark errors on scripted material, for correction

This section covers

- identifying errors
- checking techniques
- proof-reading skills
- checking by calculator
- correction marks
- marking up documents.

The **image** which your company presents to the public is very important if it is to attract new customers and keep existing customers satisfied.

A good image is maintained by
- dealing with all telephone calls promptly and courteously
- giving visitors immediate attention
- keeping reception areas and offices clean and well decorated
- providing good service and producing high quality goods
- ensuring that all correspondence and other documentation sent out from the company is well presented, clear and accurate.

This means proof-reading and checking *all* typed and printed documents carefully.

Identifying errors

Look back at the list of spellings on pages **37** and **38** and read through the section on punctuation on pages **39–41**.

See if you can find *one* spelling error and *one* punctuation error in *each* of the following sentences.

1 The commitee will make a decision in one weeks time.

2 Special items of mail should be kept seperate from franked mail?

3 Many items of stock can be ordered from catologues and this method is used by many companies

4 Accomodation in Venice Rome, Florence and Milan was arranged by the travel company.

5 Can you name two occassions when it would not be suitable to wear jeans.

Checking techniques

When typing up documents from manuscript, be on the lookout for obvious errors such as the following:

- ... visit you on Thursday, 24 May – *shouldn't this be Thursday, 25 May?*
- ... the amount owing is £270.95 (£234 + VAT @ 17½ %) – *shouldn't this be £274.95?*
- ... confirm our reservation for five nights, 16–19 July inclusive – *shouldn't this be four nights?*
- ... and whilst I am in Lancashire, I hope to visit Altrincham – *isn't Altrincham in Cheshire?*
- ... the Company are sure you will understand – *shouldn't this be 'the Company **is** sure'?*

If you are uncertain about the accuracy of anything in a document, you *must* check with the person who gave it to you.

Always

- read through *typed* documents before taking the page from your machine – it is far easier to alter errors.
- proof-read your VDU screen carefully and check pagination before printing
- use a ruler when checking columns of figures
- ask another person to read important documents to you to make sure you have not omitted a line.

Proof-reading skills

There are several types of error which you should be on the lookout for
- spelling • grammatical • spacing • punctuation • layout.

Can you find five errors in each of the following paragraphs?

1 Michael was looking forward very much to his first day at Collage has he knew the qual-ifications which he had achieved would help   him to progress atwork.

2 If most ofyour money is in a building society, A fall in intrest rates can only mean a drop on your standard of living

3 Most children watch television for atleast four hours each day? It as been sugested that this is the reason for the fall in reading standard.

4 The heaviest snowfall usually occurs in Febuary allthough heavy fall have been known to occur in march. I can remember a particularly bad year when i was a child.

Have you found them all?

Checking by calculator

Use a calculator to check the following.

Make a note of those which are incorrect.

1 There were 47 items priced at £4.95 each, making a total of £323.65.

2 The suite is £1015.79 (£864.50 + VAT @ 17½%)

3 The price of the goods is £1003.80, payable by 12 equal monthly instalments of £83.65.

4 Your deposit of 20% has been deducted from the purchase price of £235, leaving a balance owing of £88.

5 If the balance of £750 is paid within 7 days, a discount of 5%, amounting to £37 can be deducted.

Correction marks

If you are working towards a typing examination, you should be familiar with the various symbols which indicate that corrections need to be made to a document.

These signs are also used to mark up incorrect documents in business offices. Look through the main correction signs shown in the chart below.

Sign	Meaning
~~and the~~	delete these words
your ⟨front⟩ office	insert the word 'front'
yester͜ day	close up
the document. ⌐Today	both signs indicate a new paragraph
//Today	
... will be expected. ⌐ I shall be	run on – do not start a new paragraph
white ⁀and⁀ black	transpose – should be 'black and white'
rec⁀ei⁀pt	'receipt'
ⓤⓒ simon Carter	uc = upper case – change to a capital letter
ⓛⓒ all the Colleges	lc = lower case – change to a small letter
✓ ~~the child~~ (stet)	stet – retain the struck-through words
are to include all details (relevant)	insert ballooned word(s) where indicated
to⟋the	leave a space

Draft documents are usually typed in double-line spacing to make correcting easier.

Read through the following letter which has been marked with correction symbols.

Type an accurate copy of the letter following these correction marks.

Mrs Clare Hindle
516 Park͜hurst Lane
GLASGOW
G71 0XD

⟨Single spacing⟩

⟨13 September 199-⟩

ᴜᴄ Dear madam

We are un͜able to supply /the pattern which you ordered because it is temporarily out of stock. We enclose a ⟨label⟩ replacement for the one which you ~~has~~ have used and would suggest you re-order the correct ~~pattern~~ stet from our latest Catalogue. ʟᴄ

The cost of your replace͜ment pat⟨t⟩ern should /not exceed the price originally paid.

⌐Please return your order to us, using the enclosed pre-paid envelope.

Yours faithfully

P Mason
Director

Encs

56

Marking up documents

Sometimes you may be asked to check a document. You will be expected to use the previously mentioned symbols to indicate the corrections required.

Remember

✔ Mark the errors clearly.

✔ indicate the correction in the margin alongside if there is not enough room in the text.

✔ Use a different coloured pen, preferably red, so that the corrections will show clearly.

✔ Take extra care when checking numbers, dates and calculations.

✔ To avoid confusion, keep to a consistent layout.

> Your tutor will give you a notice about cruising (page 150). Check through this document carefully for errors in spelling, grammar, punctuation or layout. Mark all errors clearly with a red pen.

Section review

Rewrite or type the following sentences correctly.

1 Correction sign's should always be marked with a different colored pen.

2 Errors could be in punctuation, spelling grammer or layout.

3 all numerical data should be checked for accuracy and any errors or ommisions identified.

4 It is preferably that two people check a document- one reading and the other checking.

5 Errors should be brought to the attention of the author and amendment if neccesary.

6 The Image of the company can be spoiled by badly presented documents

7 If your spelling is pooor, you should use the spell check onyour word proccessor.

8 When typing documents, al-ways read through for error's before taking the page from your typewriter.

9 A dictionery shouldbe used if your spelling is not to good.

10 It is sensible to use a Ruler when checking documents contain-ing   figures?

3.3 Update records in a computerised database

This section covers

- what is a database?
- database records
- entering data
- advantages of electronic filing
- amending and updating records

- planning and organising work
- disk copying and back-up
- care of floppy disks
- security and confidentiality
- reporting system faults.

What is a database?

There are two methods of keeping information on record.

Manual system

Details are handwritten or typed on cards. The cards are then sorted into the required order and kept in a card index box or tray, to be referred to when needed. (Look back at page **9** – index cards.)

Electronic system

Information is input into a computer and the details are then stored onto disk to be recalled as and when required. This method of storage is called a **database**.

Note: Information stored on disk is often referred to as **data**.

Database records

The type of information you may wish to keep in a database could include

- customer records
- student records
- employee records
- library books
- plants stocked by a garden centre.

A typical employee record card would probably look like this.

```
┌─────────────────────────────────────────────────────────────────────┐
│  EMPLOYEE RECORD                                                       │
│                                                                       │
│  SURNAME_____   FIRST NAME _____   M/F __             │
│  ADDRESS _____            │
│                                                                       │
│  _____         │
│  _____  POSTCODE_____              │
│  TEL NO _____  DATE OF BIRTH _____                 │
│  DEPARTMENT _____  DATE JOINED _____                 │
│  STARTING SALARY _____  DATE LEFT _____                 │
└─────────────────────────────────────────────────────────────────────┘
```

Employee information is keyed into the blank spaces.

These spaces are referred to as **fields** and can be designed to the number of spaces required.

Entering data

A company transferring its employee records from a manual card index to a database system will find that in the initial stages there is a lot of work involved. To input each employe record, the database operator will

- bring a blank record to the screen
- key in the employee details to the respective fields
- check that all the entries are accurate – going back and amending any which are not
- finally, save the completed record to disk.

A large database file is generally stored on hard disk rather than floppy disk because of the volume of information.

Once all the manual records have been transferred to the database, the system is easily maintained.

Advantages of electronic filing

In one word – many!

✔ Records can be sorted and printed out in many different ways

    eg   alphabetical
         gender (male or female)
         department
         age
         joining date
         salary.

    (Print-outs are called **reports**.)

✔ Records are sorted within seconds.
✔ Disk storage space is considerably less than that needed for a manual card system.
✔ Details on each record can easily be updated

    eg   change of address
         transfer of department.

✔ Records for new employees can easily be added.
✔ Records are quickly deleted for employees who have left.

Amending and updating records

Always

- Check that you are amending the correct record. There may be more than one record for popular names such as John Brown, Alan Jones or Salma Patel.

    Make sure you have selected the correct one by checking the address or age.

- Before storing to disk, double-check that the information you have entered is correct and that *all* relevant fields have been completed.

    Note: The amended record is saved in place of the old one.

Your tutor has set up a database for employee records (see suggested record on p151).

1 Input the employee details shown below. Check that all information on each record is accurate before storing to disk.

2 Upon completion, sort the records into alphabetical order and take a print-out for your file.

3 Select all employees who work in the Sales Department and print out one copy for your file.

4 Three of the employee records need updating. Amend these, save and take a print-out of the three amended records for your file.

- Kathleen Ford has moved house. Her new address is 5 Appleby Close, Preston, PR2 5FG. Her telephone number is now 642198.
- Peter Gorse has changed his address to 325 School Lane, Preston, PR4 2DC. His telephone number remains the same.
- Sarah Eccles has moved from Admin to Accounts.

EMPLOYEE RECORDS TO BE INPUT INTO DATABASE

Name	Address	Tel no	DoB	Department	Date joined	Starting salary
Mr William Slater	50 Clough Road, Preston, PR4 5JK	686432	26.02.48	Sales	14.03.84	£12 900
Mrs Julie Boardman	214 Kent Court, Preston, PR1 3JM	731284	13.11.53	Accounts	21.06.88	£12 000
Miss Pamela Taylor	4 Cornwall Road, Preston, PR2 7KK	432165	21.04.57	Admin	01.09.87	£10 550
Mr Hanif Qureshi	78 Green Lane, Preston, PR2 1SX	642139	23.11.70	Admin	11.10.89	£12 650
Mrs Susan Parker	413 Grove Street, Preston, PR3 7MN	325911	13.01.60	Accounts	12.04.87	£9900
Mr Adam Patel	74 Cherry Street, Preston, PR2 6GF	553554	27.10.69	Sales	03.02.89	£9500
Miss Kathleen Ford	15 Park Road, Preston, PR3 5FF	742139	01.06.61	Admin	14.12.88	£12 400
Mr Thomas McGuire	321 Rutland Way, Preston, PR4 7LP	663844	12.04.70	Sales	15.10.90	£11 350
Mrs Jean Radcliffe	43 Alder Drive, Preston, PR2 4DW	342896	12.12.69	Sales	01.08.88	£10 000
Mr David Ryder	3 St Annes Drive Preston, PR4 2BB	652563	14.09.68	Accounts	12.10.89	£9900
Mr Paul Lambert	15 Hampshire Road, Preston, PR2 9NB	743759	15.10.65	Sales	15.09.89	£10 400
Mrs Jennifer Cooper	435 Branch Road, Preston, PR3 8WQ	663612	12.02.66	Accounts	01.02.87	£14 600
Miss Faroza Lorgat	5 Brindle Way, Preston, PR2 1XC	325981	15.03.73	Accounts	12.11.90	£8250
Mr Gary Jones	50 Lynwood Place, Preston, PR1 5DC	624139	21.12.65	Sales	14.03.89	£9900
Mr Peter Gorse	4 Church Road, Preston, PR3 9TY	553891	03.01.68	Admin	18.07.88	£13 600
Miss Sarah Eccles	58 May Terrace, Preston, PR3 5YT	432817	22.12.67	Admin	22.03.88	£12 200
Mr Carl Haworth	289 Clarence Street, Preston, PR2 5KM	699812	30.12.66	Sales	24.08.89	£14 700
Miss Janet Keen	34 Stanley Street, Preston, PR4 6QA	213312	13.11.71	Admin	22.05.88	£10 500
Mr John Sykes	14 Meadow Road, Preston, PR1 5GB	349614	19.10.63	Accounts	27.04.90	£14 400

Planning and organising work

If one of your duties is to maintain a database

- Try to set aside a regular time each day or week for inputting or amending records.
- Do not let work build up or it will become a mammoth task to clear the backlog.
- Keep records confidential by making sure your VDU screen is not visible to other staff.
- If print-out reports are wanted by colleagues, make sure that you keep to the deadline requested.

'It's all right, Mrs Pearson, I'm just keeping my records confidential!'

Disk copying and back up

Disasters can happen and one of the worst would be if you were unable to access the records in your database because of disk error or damage to a disk.

You must make a habit of copying your work onto a back-up disk each day. If you have stored to hard disk, you will probably need to copy on to more than one floppy disk.

Ideally, the back-up disks should be kept in a separate area from the original in case of fire.

Care of floppy disks

Disks are easily damaged. Look after them by

- writing the label before attaching it to the disk to avoid pressure on sensitive areas
- keeping all disks in dust jackets when they are not being used
- not handling the exposed magnetic areas on 5¼" disks
- storing disks upright in a special disk box and not packing too many in a box
- not letting the disks come into contact with magnetic surfaces or objects as this may wipe off data
- not storing disks near heat or in sunlight.

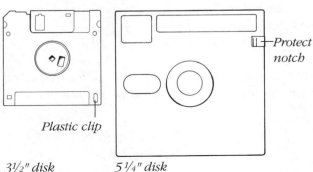

Plastic clip

3½" disk

—*Protect notch*

5¼" disk

Prevent anyone accidentally overwriting your disk by

- covering the read/write protect notch with a tab sticker on 5¼" disks
- moving the protective plastic clip on 3½" disks.

Security and confidentiality

A password, only given to certain employees, can prevent unauthorised access to records in a database. The password should be changed frequently.

Note: Passwords do not appear on screen when typed, thus preventing them being seen by other people.

Because many databases contain confidential information, do not leave print-outs lying around. Ensure that discarded print-outs are **shredded** and not just thrown into a waste paper bin.

Do not leave a record on screen for others to see whilst you leave the room.

Information obtained whilst using a database must not be passed on to anyone else.

The **Data Protection Act 1984** states that
- companies holding employee data on computer must register as data users
- information held on computer must be obtained legally
- personal data must not be given to other people
- all data must be kept up to date and be accurate
- companies must ensure that unauthorised access, alteration or destruction is not permitted
- personal records must not be kept any longer than necessary.

Persons are entitled under the Act to
- obtain a list of holders of data by applying to the Data Protection Registrar
- write to the holder of the data requesting a copy of personal information held.

Note: A fee of approximately £10 is charged for this.

Reporting system faults

Sometimes your computer, VDU or keyboard will not work.

Before sending for help, make the following checks on the equipment.
- Is the power switched on?
- Is everything plugged in properly?
- Have you switched on the on/off switch?
- Is the connection between the computer and the VDU secure?
- Has anyone turned the brightness down on the VDU screen, resulting in a blank screen?
- Is the connection between the computer and the keyboard secure?
- Have you inserted a disk in the disk drive?
- Is the disk inserted the correct way round?
- Remove the disks, switch off, leave for 30 seconds, then try again.
- Refer to the computer manual.

If you are still unable to discover the fault, you will have to ask for help. Try to be specific about the exact problem you are experiencing. Do not just say, 'It won't work!'

Section review

Fill in the missing letters, then write the words in your folder to help you remember them.

1 An electronic system of filing record cards is called a _a_a_a_e.

2 The spaces for completing information on a record card are called f___ds.

3 Information kept in a database can be s_r__d quickly.

4 A print-out of database records is called a r_p_rt.

5 To prevent losing work which has been stored to disk a __ck-_p copy should always be made.

6 A __ss__rd will prevent unauthorised persons from accessing your database.

7 Under the __t_ ___t_ct__n Act, employees can request a copy of personal information kept on a database.

8 Disks stored near h___ may become damaged.

9 If your computer will not work, you must first check all __nn_c_io__.

10 Covering the read/write protect notch on 5¼" disks will prevent anyone from ov__w__t__g your files.

WORDSEARCH

Look at the grid shown below and find the following words.

ELECTRONIC
RECORD
DATABASE
PRINTOUT
REPORT
DISK
BACKUP
FAULTS
VDU
PASSWORD

E	X	E	O	Y	U	P	T	L	W	N
B	L	K	H	M	Q	L	T	J	K	P
W	V	E	D	F	T	U	U	V	D	U
A	C	H	C	O	O	E	T	E	I	K
F	A	U	L	T	S	Z	U	P	S	C
W	Q	P	N	J	R	D	F	G	K	A
E	R	I	R	E	P	O	R	T	O	B
H	R	E	C	O	R	D	N	N	E	W
P	A	S	S	W	O	R	D	I	P	R
V	B	W	R	H	J	I	R	E	C	Q
V	L	Y	D	A	T	A	B	A	S	E

4 Processing petty cash and invoices

4.1 Process petty cash transactions

This section covers

- what petty cash is used for
- security
- imprest system
- petty cash vouchers
- balancing petty cash
- irregularities
- recording vouchers.

What petty cash is used for

Most offices find that they need to make **cash** payments each day for items bought for the office, eg cleaning materials, light bulbs, tea, coffee, flowers and plants.

Instead of asking the chief cashier each time cash is required, it is simpler to make these payments from **petty cash**.

The petty cash is an amount of money made up of small notes and coins. This cash is kept in a lockable metal cash box.

Coins are kept in the removable cash tray with notes placed safely underneath the tray.

A lockable cash box

Security

For security, the cash box is kept either in the safe or in a locked cupboard.

The box is *never* left on a desk unattended.

It is sensible to have only one set of keys for the cash box and these keys are generally looked after by an accounts clerk or a senior secretary. This person would also be called the **petty cashier**.

'I think the petty cash box is quite safe, Mrs Pearson!'

Can you think of a reason why this sum of money is called 'petty cash'? Those of you with some knowledge of the French language may know!

Can you think of any other cash payments which would be made out of the petty cash? What about people who provide a regular service to your office each week and need to be paid?

Imprest system

The amount of money kept in the petty cash box is usually known as the **imprest** amount and will vary within each office. It could range from £20 in a small office to as much as £1000 in a large organisation where many petty cash payments are made each day.

Petty cash vouchers

Whenever an employee wishes to claim back money which has been spent on items for the office, they should complete a **petty cash voucher** with details of the items purchased and the price paid. Receipts should always be obtained for these items and attached to the petty cash voucher as proof of purchase. If more than one item has been purchased, the amounts are totalled on the voucher to show the full amount being claimed. The voucher should be dated and signed by the person claiming the money.

To prevent employees claiming money for items which are not essential (or have not actually been purchased!), a supervisor should **authorise** (give permission for) each claim by signing the voucher as well.

Look at the voucher below which Sally Crossley has completed. Her office manager, Paula Denton, has authorised this purchase.

Sally has kept the receipts to attach to the voucher as proof of purchase.

A voucher would also be completed by the petty cashier before making payments to people who were being paid for a service they had given the company eg milkman, cleaner, window cleaner.

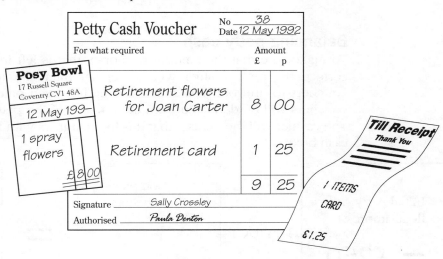

 Why do you think it is important that a voucher is completed and signed before money is given from the petty cash box?

The petty cashier will check that the voucher has been correctly completed (dated, added up correctly, signed, authorised), and is supported by receipts for the purchases.

The petty cashier numbers the vouchers, in order, and they are filed in numerical order. Usually, they are kept in the petty cash box. The correct cash can then be handed over to the person making the claim.

All completed vouchers must be kept with the petty cash box as they will be needed at a later date when the petty cash is checked and balanced.

Your tutor will give you *four* blank petty cash vouchers (page 152).

Complete one for each day for the following items purchased by you.

Where more than one item has been purchased on the same day, you should total these on the voucher.

Do not forget to sign each voucher. (Your tutor will also sign to authorise payment.)

Note that each voucher has been given a consecutive (following) number by the petty cashier.

Date	Voucher number	Items bought	Amount
21 May 199–	112	1 box 5¼" computer disks	£7.20
23 May 199–	113	Sandwiches for directors' lunch meeting	£11.50
		2 cartons of orange drink	1.90
24 May 199–	114	Fee for special delivery letter	£2.04
		Fee for mailing parcel	5.20
25 May 199–	115	Desk polish	£2.50
		Duster	1.40

Balancing petty cash

To make sure that the amount of money that is left in the petty cash box is correct, the petty cashier will, at regular intervals, add up the petty cash vouchers to find out how much money has been paid out. The total of the vouchers will be deducted from the amount of the petty cash float (imprest). The cashier will then check that this figure agrees with the money in the petty cash box.

Initial petty cash float (imprest) = £250	DEDUCT	 Completed vouchers = £63	=	Cash remaining in petty cash box £187

Irregularities

There may be times when the amount remaining in the petty cash box does not balance. These occasions are called **irregularities**.

Can you think of any reasons why the remaining petty cash would not agree with the vouchers?

Reasons could include:
- The cash has been counted wrongly.
- Voucher(s) could be missing.
- The vouchers have been totalled incorrectly.
- The petty cashier has handed out too much or too little cash in error.
- An error has been made when deducting the total of the vouchers from the original imprest.
- *Money has been stolen from the petty cash box!*

Did you think of all these reasons?

If, after checking all the above suggestions, the amount of petty cash remaining is still incorrect, a senior person should be told immediately so that the matter can be checked further.

'Can you find the error, Mrs Pearson?'

Recording vouchers

Each week or month, the petty cashier will enter details of each voucher in the **petty cash book**, recording the various amounts paid out under column headings. These columns are called **analysis columns**.

The headings will vary from firm to firm but typical columns could include **postage**, **entertaining**, **office expenses** and **cleaning**.

See below how the petty cash vouchers which you completed earlier would be recorded in the analysis columns.

PETTY CASH BOOK

Date	Details	No	Total amount	Postage	Entertaining	Office expenses	Cleaning
			£ p	£ p	£ p	£ p	£ p
21 May	5¼" computer disks	112	7.20			7.20	
23 May	Sandwiches/ orange drink	113	13.40		13.40		
24 May	Special delivery letter and parcel	114	7.24	7.24			
25 May	Polish/duster	115	3.90				3.90

To make sure that the money remaining in the petty cash box is correct, you should now carry out the following tasks.

Task 1 Total each of the *five* columns in the above petty cash book and insert your answers in the boxes below.

£ [   ] = £ [   ] + £ [   ] + £ [   ] + £ [   ]

Task 2 Check that the total of the left-hand box above equals the sum of the remaining four boxes.

Task 3 Deduct the amount paid out in vouchers (this is the figure shown above in the left-hand box) from the original petty cash float of £150 and insert your answer in the box opposite.

£ [   ]

Task 4 Calculate the value of the following notes and coins which remain in the petty cash box and total where indicated.

		£	p
3 × £10 notes	=	....	
3 × £5 notes	=	....	
46 × £1 coins	=	....	
49 × 50p coins	=	....	
7 × 20p coins	=	....	
6 × 10p coins	=	....	
13 × 5p coins	=	....	
4 × 2p coins	=	....	
3 × 1p coins	=	....	
TOTAL	=	£ [ ]	

Does your total figure in task 4 agree with your answer to task 3?

It should! If not, check back to see where you have made an error.

Section review

Fill in the missing letters and then write the completed words in your folder to help you remember them.

1 A petty cash voucher should be completed for each tr_ns_ct__n.

2 The petty cashier will pr_c_s_ all petty cash vouchers.

3 Purchases made from petty cash must be s__po_t_d by receipts.

4 Each petty cash purchase must be au__or_s_d by a receipt.

5 for s__ur_ty reasons, the petty cash box must be kept locked at all times.

6 The amount of cash beginning each petty cash period is known as the imp___t.

7 The term given to those occasions when the petty cash does not balance is ir__g_lar_t__s.

8 All vouchers are r_cord__ by the petty cashier in the petty cash book.

9 The column headings in the petty cash book are referred to as a___ys_s columns.

10 When handling cash, safety pr_c_d_r_s must always be followed.

WORDSEARCH

Look at the grid shown below and find the following words.

IMPREST

PETTY CASHIER

ACCURATE

ANALYSIS

SECURITY

IRREGULARITY

SAFETY

AUTHORISE

TRANSACTION

VOUCHER

D	F	H	K	W	S	E	C	U	R	I	T	Y	Q
Q	X	T	U	V	D	K	L	A	R	E	T	F	D
N	P	E	T	T	Y	C	A	S	H	I	E	R	T
O	D	V	C	M	I	Y	R	C	R	K	H	B	C
I	D	C	Q	V	H	A	N	A	L	Y	S	I	S
T	Q	C	X	Z	O	K	L	F	Y	W	A	B	O
C	S	I	P	Q	A	U	T	H	O	R	I	S	E
A	N	B	X	P	G	C	C	Q	J	K	D	E	W
S	S	A	F	E	T	Y	C	H	E	T	Y	J	K
N	A	G	R	K	Y	Y	N	U	E	P	L	G	D
A	V	R	Y	N	X	J	M	R	R	R	J	L	U
R	I	M	P	R	E	S	T	F	S	A	D	A	L
T	E	W	D	J	C	O	T	P	A	X	T	T	E
G	B	Q	Y	U	M	L	P	S	Z	F	B	E	T

4.2 Process incoming invoices for payment

This section covers

- documents used in buying and selling
- delivery notes
- goods received notes (GRN)
- invoices
  - discounts
  - VAT
  - delivery charges
- checking invoices
- reporting errors and discrepancies
- passing invoices for payment
- liaison between Purchasing, Sales and Accounts departments.

Documents used in buying and selling

There are a number of different types of business documents which pass between companies when they buy goods from one another.

Look at the chart below which illustrates the order in which these documents are used.

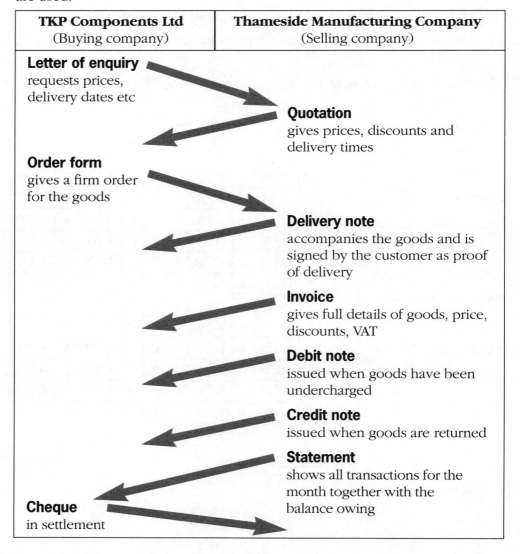

TKP Components Ltd (Buying company)	Thameside Manufacturing Company (Selling company)

Letter of enquiry
requests prices, delivery dates etc

Quotation
gives prices, discounts and delivery times

Order form
gives a firm order for the goods

Delivery note
accompanies the goods and is signed by the customer as proof of delivery

Invoice
gives full details of goods, price, discounts, VAT

Debit note
issued when goods have been undercharged

Credit note
issued when goods are returned

Statement
shows all transactions for the month together with the balance owing

Cheque
in settlement

Delivery notes

When goods are delivered by the supplier, the person receiving the goods (usually someone from the Stores Department), is asked to sign a **delivery note** as proof of receipt.

The person signing for the goods must make the following checks:
- That the goods delivered are as listed on the delivery note. (If the goods are securely packed in boxes, and it is not possible to check the contents, a note would be made that 'five boxes were received'.)
- That the goods are received in a satisfactory condition. (Any damage would be recorded on the delivery note.)

The delivery note is then returned to the driver of the van, with a copy being retained by the buyer for future reference.

Goods received note (GRN)

Many firms now record details of all incoming goods on computer and current stock balances are adjusted automatically. Usually a **goods received note** (GRN), which gives detailed information of the goods received is produced by the computer. These goods are linked up with the original **order** for the goods.

A copy of the GRN is then passed to the **Accounts Department** so that details of the goods received can be checked against the invoice which is received from the supplier a few days later.

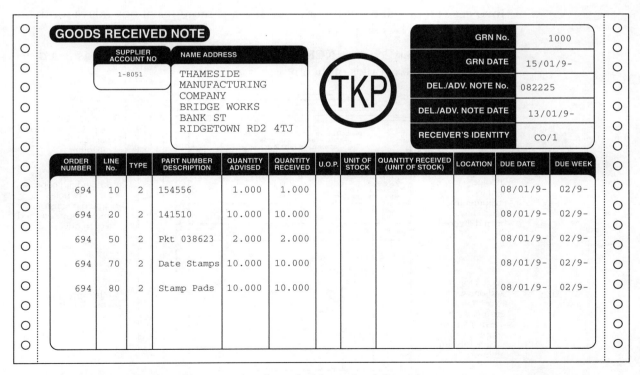

Goods received note produced by computer from details on the delivery note

Firms which do not operate computerised stock control may record details of deliveries manually on a **goods received sheet**.

(TKP)	GOODS RECEIVED SHEET					Sheet No. ......496......	
Customer	Customer Advice No.	T K P Order No.	Date Received	Description of goods		Quantity	Part or Complete
J. W. ENTWISTLE	1673	N/K	7/10/9-	INJECTION MOULD TOOL		1	
LAMBERT CLEANING	PO93	11675	"	HARD SURFACE CLEANER ODEX		12	
T. K. MARSDEN	36164	VERBAL	"	ROCOL FLAW FINDER CLEANER		1	T11308
" "	"	"	"	PENOTRAUNT		1	~
" "	"	"	"	DEVELOPER		1	~
" "	35752	11874	"	8" IROCA ADJ		1	T11309
" "	"	"	"	3M STANLEY TAPE		1	~
" "	"	"	"	TOOL BOX TB 1750		1	~
VULCAN ENG	61707	11799	"	3M8709 MASKS		30	T10072
" "	3264	–	"	RADIATOR GRILLE TOOL		1	~
SIMPSON BROS	16329	11801	"	RIGGER GLOVES		6 PRS	T10470
" "	"	"	"	12" NELSON HEAD SEMI STIFF		6	~
" "	"	"	"	SOFT BANNISTER BRUSH		6	~
" "	"	"	"	1" PAINT BRUSH		6	~
" "	16384	11624	"	NO 2 SQ MOUTH SHOVEL		2	T10461

Goods received sheet written manually from details on the delivery note

Invoices

The supplier now sends a bill to the buyer for the goods delivered. This is called an **invoice**.

Invoices can be handwritten or typed but it is more usual nowadays for them to be produced by computer.

Special stationery, using **NCR** paper (**no carbon required**) is used to produce up to *six* copies of the invoice.

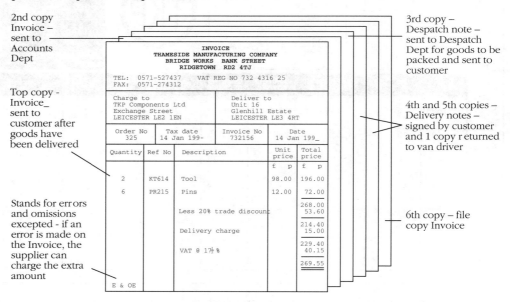

2nd copy Invoice – sent to Accounts Dept

3rd copy – Despatch note – sent to Despatch Dept for goods to be packed and sent to customer

Top copy - Invoice sent to customer after goods have been delivered

4th and 5th copies – Delivery notes – signed by customer and 1 copy returned to van driver

Stands for errors and omissions excepted - if an error is made on the Invoice, the supplier can charge the extra amount

6th copy – file copy Invoice

Note: The price of the goods together with discounts, delivery charges and VAT is not shown on the **Despatch note** or the **Delivery notes**.

Different coloured copies are used for easy identification of the various documents.

Discounts

There are *two* types of discount which can be given by the supplier.

- **Trade discount** is given to buyers who are 'in the trade' or who buy goods in bulk. It is usually given as a percentage.

  eg less 20% trade discount

- **Cash discount** is given to encourage buyers to pay for goods promptly, a small extra discount is offered to those who settle their account within, say 7 days.

  eg Terms: 2½% within 7 days

Suppliers offer both types of discount to customers.

Value added tax (VAT)

This is a tax which is charged on most business sales. It is added after *all* discounts have been deducted.

The current rate (which is set by the Government and can be changed by them) is 17½ per cent.

Delivery charges

Some companies make a charge for delivering goods to the buyer. This charge is added to the invoice. VAT is payable on any delivery charges.

Checking invoices

The Accounts Department who check all invoices usually follow this procedure.

- If VAT has been added to the invoice, check that the VAT registration number is shown on the invoice.

- Check that the invoice is actually addressed to your company, not addressed to someone else and sent to you in error!

- Check for a **valid** order number or the identifying name of the person who ordered the goods – employees could order goods for themselves!

- Check the quantity, description of the goods and price against that on the purchase order.

- Check that the goods have actually been received – have you got a GRN? Some companies are rather too quick at sending invoices!

- Check that the quantity and description of the goods agrees with that on the GRN. It is possible that only part of an order has been sent!

- Finally, check all calculations for accuracy. Has the discount been taken off and the VAT added on, and not vice versa?

Use your calculator to work out the cost of the following goods:

1 1 reclining chair @ £385 + VAT @ 17½%

2 24 china tea sets @ £83.60 each + VAT @ 17½%

3 36 metres of carpet @ £18.50 per metre, less 25% trade discount, with VAT @ 17½%

4 12 table lamps @ £37.85 each, less 10% trade discount with VAT @ 17½%

5 20 video recorders @ £426.95 each, less 35% trade discount, with VAT @ 17½%

Reporting errors and discrepancies

- If the description or amount charged differs from the purchase order, check with the Purchasing Department, who will contact the supplier of the goods for verification.
- If the description or quantity differs from what is on the GRN, check with the Stores Department who will turn up the delivery note to check whether they have recorded the details on the GRN correctly.

If the actual delivery note shows that insufficient goods have been delivered
  - either the buying company will issue a debit note to the supplier for the amount overcharged
  - or a credit note will be requested from the supplier.

- If goods are invoiced but a record cannot be found of receiving them, it is usual to telephone the supplier asking for **proof of delivery** (POD).
- If an error is found in the calculations, the supplier should be contacted immediately. The supplier may
  - request the buyer to alter the invoice in ink and they will make amendments to their copy
  - ask the buyer to destroy the invoice and they will issue a replacement
  - send a credit note to cancel the incorrect invoice, then issue a corrected invoice.

Check the following calculations for accuracy.

Trade discount is 15% and VAT is charged at 17½ % on all transactions.

Make a note of the correct answer for any which have been calculated wrongly.

1 36 items @ £12.50 each = £499.44

2 70 items @ £4.95 each = £346.07

3 21 items @ £216 each = £4530.33

4 9 items @ £84.50 each = £759.55

5 10 items @ £100 each = £701.25

Passing invoices for payment

Points to remember

- If the invoice ties up with the purchase order and goods received note (GRN), and the calculations are correct, it can be passed for payment.

- After checking, invoices are usually authorised for payment by a senior member of staff.
- To prevent mistakes, there should be several different people involved in the various stages of checking the invoice.
- The invoice is stamped with a rubber stamp and is initialled as it passes through the various stages of checking.

Liaison between Purchasing, Sales and Accounts departments

- The **Accounts Department** must keep the **Sales Department** informed of non-payment by customers so that goods do not continue to be supplied to bad payers!
- The **Sales Department** should be made aware by the **Accounts Department** of the credit limit of each customer so that this is not exceeded.
- The **Purchasing Department** must keep the **Accounts Department** informed of purchase prices and discounts arranged to prevent overcharging on the invoice.
- The **Sales Department** needs to liaise with the **Purchasing Department** to ensure that sufficient stocks of materials for production and re-sale are maintained to meet customers' requirements.

Section review

Complete the sentences below, using each of the following words once only.

authorised	invoices
E & OE	GRN
delivery	discount
accounts	NCR
computerised	errors

1 When goods are delivered to the Stores Department, someone should sign the _____ note as proof of delivery.

2 The Accounts Department check that the invoice description of the goods agrees with that on the _____.

3 When a company uses a _____ stock control system, stock balances are adjusted automatically.

4 Special stationery invoice sets can produce copies using _____ paper.

5 Before payment is made _____ must be checked carefully for errors and accuracy.

6 Errors and omissions excepted is abbreviated on an invoice by the initials _____.

7 There are two types of _____, trade and cash.

8 The _____ Department is usually responsible for checking invoices.

9 Calculations on invoices must be checked carefully for _____.

10 After checking, invoices are usually _____ for payment by a senior person.

5 Stock handling

5.1 Issue office materials on request and monitor stock levels

This section covers

- stock consumables
- storage of stationery items
- safety in the stock room
- issuing stock/stationery requisitions
- stock records
- re-ordering new stock (including emergency orders)
- receipt of new stock (including legislation)
- recording new stock
- stock checking (reconciliation)
- annual stock-taking
- computerised stock records.

Stock consumables

When you have become competent at carrying out routine clerical tasks, you may find that your supervisor asks you to undertake additional duties – sometimes making you responsible for certain jobs.

This generally means that your work to date has been satisfactory and your supervisor feels that you are capable of taking on extra responsibility – that of making sure the office does not run out of stationery items.

If a factory runs out of raw materials, production will automatically stop. It is equally important that offices do not run out of essential items such as paper, envelopes, typewriter ribbons etc. These items are known as **consumables** because they need replacing on a regular basis.

'I've typed all those letters like you asked, Mrs Pearson.
Can't send them out until next week 'cos we've run out of envelopes!'

What are consumables?

Can you supply the missing letters to identify the consumable items listed below?

1 A4 b__d p_p_r
2 A4 b_n_ p___r
3 l_t__r he_d p___r
4 _arb_n p___r
5 c_rd
6 l_b_ls
7 _n__l p_s
8 m_ss_g_ p_ds
9 d_c_m__t f__d_rs
10 p_nc_ls

11 ba_l _oin_ p_ns
12 c_rr__ti_n fl__d
13 adh___ve t_e
14 st_p__rs and s__pl__
15 _c_ss_rs
16 h___ p_nch__
17 r_bb__ st_m__
18 b_lld_g c__p_
19 p____ cl_ps
20 _l_st_c _ands

Can you think of any additional items to add to the above list?

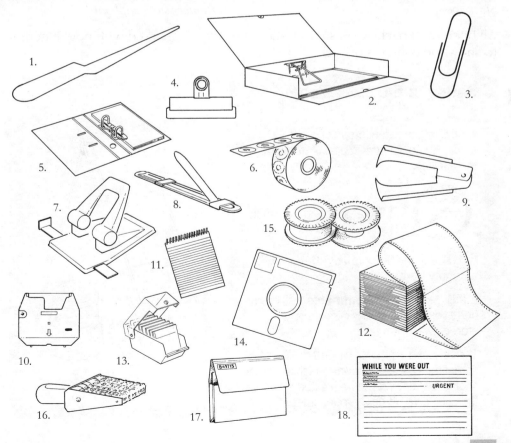

Look at the following illustrations of consumable items. can you identify them?

1.
2.
3.
4.
5.
6.
7.
8.
9.
10.
11.
12.
13.
14.
15.
16.
17.
18.

WHILE YOU WERE OUT

URGENT

Storage of stationery items

Depending upon the size of your work place, stationery is kept in either a stock room or a stationery cupboard.

 Why do you think it is important that both the stock room and stationery cupboard are kept locked at all times?

Shelves in stock rooms and stationery cupboards must be clearly labelled to show where each item can quickly be found. This will also help to identify where new stock should be placed.

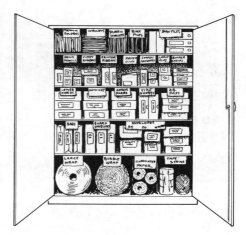

Stock room   *Stationery store cupboard*

All boxes and packets on shelves should be clearly marked with bold lettering to show the contents of each.

Safety in the stock room

Remember

! *Always* use safety steps or a safety stool when placing or reaching items from top shelves.

 ! No smoking in the stock room.

! Keep the stock room *tidy*. Throw away all empty boxes.

! Make sure that **inflammable** (will easily burn) liquids are clearly labelled and stored away from heat.

Thinners and ammonia which are sometimes used in copying machines should be kept in a well-ventilated area as they can give off dangerous fumes.

Explain to your tutor why

1 Large, bulky items should be stored either on the floor or on the bottom shelves.

2 Items requested regularly should be stored within easy reach, not on top shelves or behind other items.

3 Small items, such as erasers, correction fluid and drawing pins should be placed at the front, never behind larger items.

4 Pens and pencils should be stood upright in a box – not laid flat on shelves.

5 New stock should be placed either underneath or behind old stock.

6 Paper should always be kept in a dry, well-ventilated room, which has adequate lighting.

Issuing stock/stationery requisitions

You will almost certainly have other duties to carry out in addition to issuing stationery to staff. It is therefore more convenient to keep a regular day and time when your colleagues know they will be able to obtain supplies of stationery from the stockroom or cupboard.

This distribution can be organised in several ways:

- Each week staff can write their stationery requirements for the coming week in a stationery book which is circulated around the various offices and then returned to you.
- Staff can write a note to you listing the items they will need for the coming week. This type of note is called a **stationery requisition**. Supplies of these requisitions are kept by staff who will complete one when stationery is required. Each requisition is printed with a consecutive number.

Look below. Simon Ward has requested four calculator batteries.

STATIONERY REQUISITION

FROM *Simon Ward* DATE *23/10/199-*

DEPT *Accounts* REQ NO 621

Please supply:

Quantity	Item
4	Calculator batteries

Signed: *Simon Ward*

Approved by: *Georgia Kingston*

Simon has had to ask his departmental manager, Georgia Kingston, to approve his requisition.

Can you think of a reason why her approval is needed?

Your tutor will give you *four* blank stationery requisitions (page 153).

Complete a requisition from each of the following people who are requesting stationery items for the coming week.

Do not sign the requisitions but remember to date each one for 17 November.

Requisition No 731

from   Mark Greenwood of the Technical Dept

for   4 packets of A4 bond paper
1 box of staples

Requisition No 732

from   Sarah Longworth of the Secretarial Dept

for   5 packets of A4 bond paper
6 bottles of correction fluid
4 reams of A4 letter head paper

Requisition No 733

from   Hanif Sidat of the Sales Dept

for   8 packets of A4 bond paper

Requisition No 734

from   Jennifer Thomas of the Admin Dept

for   1 ream of A4 letter head paper
6 bottles of correction fluid
2 boxes of staples

When you have received the requisitions you can assemble the stationery orders, which staff can either collect at a specified time or you can deliver to them.

A notice displayed on the door of the stock room or stationery cupboard will remind staff of the arrangements for the issue of stationery.

Design a notice for display advising staff that stationery will be issued only on Tuesdays and Fridays between 0930 and 1030.

Requisitions must be received by you before 1600 the day before.

(Why not use a letter stencil or Letraset to design your notice? Have you any calligraphy skills? Can you design and print out a notice using your computer? It could look more professional than using free-hand skills!)

Stock records

It is important that you know exactly how much stationery there is in stock. To avoid having to count each individual item, a record card is usually kept for each stock item.

The record cards are generally kept in a card index box and filed in **alphabetical** order of stock item.

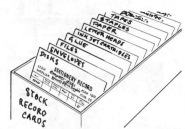

Each time an item of stationery is issued, this should be recorded on the appropriate record card.

See below how the requisition for four calculator batteries from Simon Ward as shown on page **79** is recorded on the record card.

STATIONERY RECORD CARD

ITEM: .....CALCULATOR BATTERIES.......... MAX:...100....

SUPPLIER: SUMMIT LIGHTING COMPANY MIN:...20.....

Date	Quantity received	Quantity issued	Dept	Req No	Balance in stock
1 Oct					24
23 Oct		4	Accounts	621	20

Look at the 'balance in stock' figure shown on the above record card. There are only 20 batteries left in stock, which is the minimum balance shown at the top of the card.

This serves as a reminder for you to order more batteries to prevent running out of stock. Your regular supplier of batteries is also shown at the top of the card.

Inform your tutor:

1 how many calculator batteries should be ordered to restore the balance in stock to the maximum number

2 the name of the supplier of these batteries.

Ordering too many batteries should be avoided (even if they can be purchased much more cheaply) because they
- can deteriorate in quality
- can become out of date
- tie up the firm's capital (money)
- take up valuable storage space.

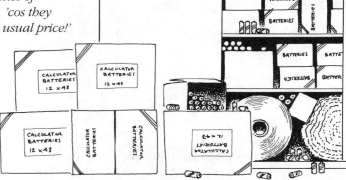

'I've ordered 10 000 boxes of batteries, Mrs Pearson, 'cos they were less than half the usual price!'

Your tutor will give you *four* stationery record cards on which have been recorded previously issued items (page 154). Each card shows the up-to-date balance in stock. Using the four requisitions which you completed earlier from the details given on page **80**, you should

1 Enter each item of stationery on to the respective record card. Calculate the up-to-date balance in stock after each entry.

2 After all four stationery requisitions have been recorded on the record cards and balances re-calculated, inform your tutor which stationery items have reached their minimum balance and therefore need re-ordering.

Have you re-calculated the balances on the stationery cards correctly?

Re-ordering new stock

Stationery can be re-ordered in either of two ways

● by sending a note of your requirements to your Purchasing Department. (This type of note is called a **purchase requisition.)** *or*
● by sending an **order form** to your usual supplier direct.

Very occasionally, stationery may need to be re-ordered in an emergency. This could occur when several departments have requested the same stock item during the same week. In this instance, telephoning the supplier would be the quickest way of receiving supplies.

Receipt of new stock

When new stock is received, this should be carefully checked for discrepancies which could mean

● missing items
● damaged items
● additional items sent in error
● incorrect items.

It is important to check that the items actually delivered match those listed on the **goods delivery note**.

If an error is discovered, the supplier should be contacted immediately so that the error can be pointed out.

Note: The **Sale of Goods Act 1979** protects buyers of goods. The legislation states that goods for sale must be

- as described
- of merchantable quality
- fit for the purpose for which they are intended.

The Trade Descriptions Act 1968 states that it is an offence to give a false description.

Recording new stock

Let us assume that we re-ordered a supply of calculator batteries when the number in stock had fallen to the minimum balance on the stationery record card, shown on page **81**. To restore the balance to the maximum number, we should have ordered 80 batteries. See how this delivery would be recorded on the record card shown below.

STATIONERY RECORD CARD

ITEM: ...CALCULATOR...BATTERIES........... MAX:..100....

SUPPLIER: SUMMIT..LIGHTING..COMPANY. MIN:..20.....

Date	Quantity received	Quantity issued	Dept	Req No	Balance in stock
1 Oct					24
23 Oct		4	Accounts	621	20
30 Oct	80				100

Using the stationery record cards previously completed by you, you should now:

1 Record the receipt of the stock items listed below on the respective record card.

Remember, all stock received is recorded in the 'quantity received' column and not the 'quantity issued' column. The new stock was received on 29 November.

Stock received
456 packets of A4 bond paper
40 boxes of staples
251 reams of A4 letter head paper

2 Calculate the up-to-date balances on each stationery record card.

Stock checking (reconciliation)

Even though an up-to-date balance of each stock item can be found on the respective stationery record card, it is important that the *actual* stock is checked at regular intervals. This check is often called an **inventory reconciliation**. Any stock which has deteriorated, been damaged or become out of date can be found during a stock check.

This stock check will also reveal whether the balances on the record cards are correct and, more important, whether any stock has been pilfered (stolen).

If any shortages (these are often called **discrepancies**) are found, the supervisor must be informed *immediately* and the matter investigated further.

Annual stock-taking

At least once a year, all stock is checked thoroughly. A list is made of all items and the value of the stock is calculated to show how much of the firm's capital is tied up in stock.

This valuation is required by the firms **auditors** who can work out how much money is being spent each year on consumable items.

Can you suggest how the firm can find out which department has been using most stationery items?

Computerised stock records

Many firms have computerised their stock records. Upon receipt, all new stock is entered into the computer and the balances are automatically adjusted.

All stationery items issued to staff are also recorded. The total amount of stock held is therefore always immediately available.

Stock-control programs quickly identify which stock needs re-ordering. However, a manual stock check must still be made once a year – sometimes more regularly.

Section review

Fill in the missing letters and then write the completed words in your folder to help you remember what they mean.

1 A note given to the stationery clerk asking for supplies of stationery is called a stationery r_qu_s_t_on.

2 An item of stationery which is used in an office and needs to be replaced regularly is called a con_____.

3 Care should be taken when storing dangerous materials in the stock room. Two words which can be used to describe these dangerous materials are haz___ous and infl__m_b__.

4 Stock which is out of date is often referred to as obs___te stock.

5 Sometimes stationery needs to be ordered very quickly because stocks are very low. The stock clerk therefore has to telephone for an em__g__c_ order.

6 The stock clerk must be aware of laws passed by the Government when receiving new stock. The laws are often referred to as leg__lat__n.

7 When checking stationery, if the balance does not agree with the balance you expect, this is called a dis____anc_.

8 Your entries on the stationery record cards should always be readable and correct. Another way of describing your writing could be leg_b__ and a__ura__.

9 Stock should be checked at regular intervals to make sure that balances are correct, that stock has not deteriorated, been stolen, damaged or become out of date. This stock check is known as a stock rec__cil_____.

10 If stock records are completed in handwriting, this is known as man___ record keeping. If stock records are recorded on a computer, this is known as com_____ised record keeping.

6 Mail handling

6.1 Receive, sort and distribute incoming/internal mail

This section covers

- receiving mail
- opening the mail
- mail-opening equipment
- recording remittances
- circulating mail (using lists)
- suspicious letters and packages.

The Post Office is now split into three separate businesses
- Royal Mail
- Royal Mail Parcelforce
- Post Office Counters Ltd.

Receiving mail

The procedure for opening the mail will depend on the size of the organisation.

In a large company, there could be a special mailroom, staffed by people whose main job is to receive incoming and despatch outgoing mail.

Many of the larger companies have a **post box number** and a messenger will collect the sacks of mail early each morning from the local sorting office instead of waiting for it to be delivered.

Other types of mail which will be dealt with will include
- internal mail – passed between departments
- parcel deliveries
- registered and recorded deliveries
- hand deliveries
- deliveries by private courier
- messages sent by fax.

In a small office, the manager or secretary will open all mail and probably deal with most of it personally.

Opening the mail

It is important that mail is opened, sorted and distributed quickly.
- Take out letters marked *private, personal* or *confidential. Do not* open these letters!
- Open letters marked *urgent* first, then first class letters, followed by second class mail.
  Printed circulars and magazines should be opened last of all.
- Deal with each letter and enclosures *before* opening the next one to prevent confusion.
- Date stamp all letters and documents. (Make sure you have changed the date on the stamp!)
- Check that all enclosures are included and either clip or staple them to the accompanying letter or document. Make a note on the document if any are missing.

- Envelopes containing remittances (payments) – cash, cheques or postal orders – should be recorded in the **remittances book** and handed to a senior person for safety.
- Sort all mail into baskets or pigeon holes for the various departments and individuals, ready for delivering or collection.
- Re-check all envelopes to make sure they are empty. It is a good idea to open all envelopes flat.
  Some firms keep these envelopes for several days in case of queries.

- Letters delivered by hand should be opened and distributed as soon as they arrive.
- Damaged parcels should not be accepted or, alternatively, should be signed for as 'damaged on delivery'.

Mail-opening equipment

Envelopes need to be opened quickly and neatly. Avoid tearing the contents.

- **A paper knife** can be used to slit open the top edge of the envelope. Take care not to tear the enclosures.
- **An electric letter opener** slices off a narrow strip from the top of each envelope. To avoid damaging the contents, envelopes should first be tapped on the desk to allow the contents to drop to the bottom.

An electric letter opener.

Recording remittances

Most organisations have some way of recording remittances received through the post.

Many firms enter details of cash, cheques and postal orders into a **remittances book**. The name of the person or firm sending the remittance is also recorded. The cashier countersigns the page when the remittances are handed over.

Name of sender	Method of payment	Amount £	p	Signature
Andrew King	Cheque	43	50	J Ryan
Cunliffe & Partners	Cheque	840	00	J Ryan
S Hunter	Cash	20	00	J Ryan
Banks & Sons Ltd	Cheque	270	90	J Ryan
P TAYLOR	CHQ	95	00	R Entwistle
M DAVIS	PO	5	00	R Entwistle

REMITTANCES BOOK DATE .... 14 September 199-....

Cashier's signature ...... K Mason ....

Your tutor will give you a page from a remittances book (page 155). The remittances listed below have been received in today's post. Enter these details on the page. Your tutor will countersign the page as cashier.

- Cheque for £426.50 from Calvert Bros – account number 67245
- Cash for £80 by registered post from K Higson – account number 23694
- £73.96 by cheque from Paul Banks – account number 32463
- Anwar Hussain sent a cheque for £32.80 – account number 34895
- Cheque for £895 from P O'Brien – account number 12423
- Registered letter containing £65 cash from S Anderson – account number 23574
- Postal order for £5 from T Dickinson – account number 43286

Circulating mail

Sometimes a letter received in the mail has to be seen urgently by more than one person.

A **distribution list** can be written neatly on the letter. The letter is then photocopied – one copy for each of the names on the distribution list. Tick the person's name to whom the copy is being sent.

Magazines and bulky reports which cannot be copied usually have a **routing** or **circulation list** attached.

CIRCULATION LIST

Name	Date rec'd	Date passed on
Simon Tate	12/6/9-	12/6/9-
M Ahmed	12/6/9-	14/6/9-
Sarah Carter	14/6/9-	
Paul O'Brien		
Lisa Carter		

Please return to Admin Manager after circulation

Suspicious letters and packages

Update on dealing with suspicious mail

! Some organisations are potential targets for this type of mail. Staff working in such places are specifically instructed to take extra care and to be diligent at all times.

! The Royal Mail letter and parcels offices have special screening equipment which scans mail.

! Information leaflets and advice on how to deal with suspicious mail can be obtained free from your local Crime Prevention Officer.

! If you receive a letter or package which causes concern, inform your supervisor or a senior person *immediately*.

Do not attempt to open the package!

Section review

Complete the sentences below, using each of the following words once only.

routing   damage
confidential   remittances
urgent   internal
sorted   suspicious
envelopes   knife

1 As well as dealing with letters which are delivered through the post, the mailroom staff also sort _____ mail.

2 Letters marked _____ should on no account be opened.

3 A paper _____ can be used to open envelopes.

4 It is wise to keep _____ for several days in case there is a need to refer to them.

5 Letters marked _____ should be opened immediately.

6 When accepting delivery of parcels, they should be checked for _____.

7 When all the mail has been opened, it should be _____ quickly into baskets or pigeon holes.

8 A circulation list is sometimes referred to as a _____ list.

9 It is wise to record all cash, cheques and postal orders in a _____ book.

10 Royal letters and parcels offices have special equipment to screen for _____ mail.

6.2 Prepare for despatch outgoing/internal mail

This section covers

- putting letters and enclosures into envelopes
- mailroom procedure
- addressing envelopes
- wrapping parcels
- Royal Mail services
- postage book
- mailroom equipment.

As soon as the incoming mail has been distributed, mailroom staff should switch their attention to the outgoing mail.

To avoid a last minute rush of mail having to be dealt with, outgoing mail should be collected at regular intervals throughout the day.

Internal mail within the organisation can be collected and distributed at the same time.

Many firms impose a final deadline for collection of outgoing mail. Nothing is more annoying than being asked to send a letter by special mail at 5 pm.

Putting letters and enclosures into envelopes

If it is the job of the mailroom staff to put letters into envelopes, care should be taken to
- check that all enclosures are attached to the letter
- check that the letter is signed
- insert the letter into the *correct* envelope, making as few folds as possible.

Window envelopes are often used nowadays and care should be taken to ensure that the name and address are fully visible. Using window envelopes avoids the error of putting a letter into the wrong envelope, and saves time.

Mailroom procedure

- Check that all envelopes are sealed. *Never* lick envelopes! Use a roller moistener to seal flaps.
- Separate all items of special mail.
- Sort mail into first and second class, keeping similar-sized envelopes together.
- Weigh any mail which feels heavier than 60g and any letters which are going abroad.
- Calculate the postage for these letters and mark the amount in pencil in one corner of the envelope.
- Complete any forms for special items of mail, then weigh and calculate the postage.
- Frank the mail or attach the correct postage stamps.
- Put franked mail in special large envelopes marked 'franked mail' ready for taking to the Post Office.

Note: Postage stamps are *always* fixed to the top right-hand corner of an envelope.

Addressing envelopes

The most popular size of envelope used in business is DL size which takes A4 paper folded equally into three.

DL envelopes are available in three styles.

  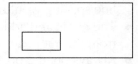

Bankers   *Pocket*   *Window*

Many firms have their name and address printed either in the left-hand corner of the envelope or on the opening flap.

An undelivered letter can quickly be returned to the sender.

Adhesive address labels are often used to stick on envelopes as these can be produced quickly by computer.

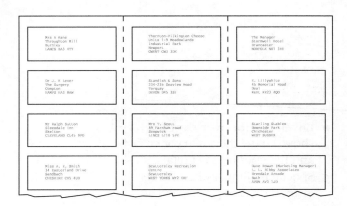

Computer address labels

Companies who use window envelopes have their letter head paper marked with two dots (or some other mark). The name and address is typed between the two marks.

When the letter is folded and inserted in the envelope, the addressee details show clearly through the window.

Ask you tutor for a window envelope and a sheet of marked letter head paper.

Type your own name and address on the letter where indicated.

Practise folding the letter and inserting it in the envelope so that your name and address is clearly visible through the window.

Rules to follow

- Make sure that the envelope is sufficiently large to take the letter *and* any enclosures.
- It is preferable to type envelopes. If handwritten, they should be neat and clear.
- On DL and smaller envelopes, use single line spacing, blocked style. Double line spacing would be clearer on larger envelopes.
- The name and address should be started halfway down and about one-third in from the left edge.
- Always put the postal town in capitals. It is preferable to put the postcode on a separate line with no punctuation. (Punctuation can slow down the Royal Mail mechanised letter sorting process.)

```
Mrs Ann Wood
31 Kay Street
CHORLEY
BB7 2KL
```

- Envelopes for overseas mail should have the town (or city) and the country in capitals.
- Special mailing and addressee instructions are positioned as shown in the illustrations below.

```
Mr John Davis

27 Fountain Avenue

CHORLEY

BB7 4FW
```

RECORDED DELIVERY

```
Mr Paul Sager
4 Ceder Avenue
MANCHESTER
M5 6YR
```

```
PERSONAL
Mr T King
464 Green Park
BIRMINGHAM
BM2 5KL
```

The same applies for registered post, special delivery and par avion (by airmail)

The same applies for personal, confidential and urgent

```
FOR THE ATTENTION OF MR T DAY
Messrs Crabtree & Page
16 High Street
EDINBURGH
EH1 4PL
```

```
Express Orders Ltd
FREEPOST
Canterbury House
EDINBURGH
EH2 5WS
```

Ask your tutor for a selection of different-sized envelopes. Folded A4 paper could be used as a substitute.

Prepare envelopes, preferably typed, for the following addresses. Start a new line where two spaces have been left between items.

For special mailing and addressee instructions check the layout with the illustrations on page 92.

1 Mrs Pauline Butterworth   Alston & Company   44 Butler Street   NORWICH   Norfolk   NR2 6QR

2 Dr David Hanson   Brierfield Health Centre   Stanley Street   EDINBURGH   EH16 5BU

3 Studio 72   Ramsgreave House   York Road   GRANTHAM   Lincs   NG3 6RZ

4 Mr B Atherton   15 Junction Road   PRESTON   Lancs   PR3 9TX
   (Mark the envelope SPECIAL DELIVERY)

5 Leisure Wear Ltd   27 Deansgate   MANCHESTER   M4 3ES
   (Mark the envelope FOR THE ATTENTION OF MR JACK CLAYTON)

6 Mr Stuart Kendal   Lincoln Chambers   47 Main Street   LONDON   SW6 3PR
   (Mark the envelope CONFIDENTIAL)

7 The Manager   Associated Systems Ltd   546 Planet Road   FARNBOROUGH   Hants   GU14 7NU
   (Mark the envelope URGENT)

Wrapping parcels

The mailroom should keep a selection of the following materials for wrapping parcels:

brown paper
strong cardboard boxes
assorted size jiffy (padded) bags
bubble wrap
corrugated paper

polystyrene chips
a supply of old newspapers
adhesive tape (various widths)
string
scissors

Rules to follow

- Use stout card to protect photographs, certificates etc.
- Jiffy bags are quick and handy for sending unbreakable items such as books.
- Wrap fragile articles first with one of the wrapping materials listed above, before placing them in a cardboard box. Make sure the articles can withstand bumps and rough handling.
- Secure the box with generous adhesive tape or string.
- Label the parcel clearly, following the layout rules for addressing letters on page **92**.
- Put the sender's name and address on the outside of the parcel in case it cannot be delivered for some reason.

Royal Mail services

There are a number of different ways of sending letters, packets and parcels through the post. The main services are listed below.

Letter post

- **First class post** – delivered the day after collection
- **Second class post** – delivered by the third working day after collection
- **Certificate of posting** – gives proof of posting only

Priority services

For speed

- Special delivery – next day delivery
- Express delivery – next day delivery (including Isle of Man and CI)
- Datapost – next day delivery

For security

- Registered post – to send money/valuables

For signature on delivery

- Recorded delivery – to send *important* documents (not valuables)

For proof of delivery

- Advice of delivery – proof of delivery returned to sender – can be used with registered or recorded delivery mail.

Reply services

- Business reply service – customers can reply without paying for postage – envelopes or postcards are printed with a special design showing licence number.

- Freepost – again saves customers paying for postage – Freepost is included in the address.

International

- Airmail – to send mail abroad quickly. Lightweight mail to EC countries will go at a special rate. Outside Europe – use an Airmail label or write 'PAR AVION – BY AIRMAIL' on envelope
- Swiftair – for sending urgent mail abroad quickly. Pre-paid envelopes called SWIFTPACKS now available to send anywhere in the world.
- Datapost – a very fast service for sending mail abroad
- Airstream – for companies who send large quantities of mail abroad.

Parcels

- Parcelforce datapost – guaranteed next morning delivery
- Parcelforce 24 – guaranteed next day delivery
- Parcelforce 48 – guaranteed delivery within 2 days
- Parcelforce standard – normally delivered within 2-3 working days
- Compensation Fee parcel – to send valuable parcels

There are other **private carriers** who will deliver parcels.

Details can be found in *Yellow Pages* under 'Courier Services'.

British Rail Red Star offer an ordinary station-to-station next day parcel delivery service, or a more expensive same day delivery for urgent parcels.

As a group, obtain the following booklets from the Royal Mail.

- *UK Letter Rates – A Comprehensive Guide*
- *Royal Mail International – A comprehensive mailing guide for business users*
- *Parcelforce – The power to deliver nationwide*

Use these booklets to find more detailed information on the Royal Mail services listed above.

Up-to-date charges are given for the mailing services.

Postage book

Although many firms now have franking machines for stamping the outgoing mail, smaller offices still use postage stamps. A record therefore should be kept of all outgoing mail together with the cost of postage.

Because of the volume of first and second class letters, this type of mail is batched and recorded in the **postage book** as '56 1st class letters' or '23 2nd class letters'.

Details of special mail, however, is recorded in the book together with the value of stamps used. Additional fees for special mail are usually taken from petty cash. Receipts obtained from the Post Office are generally clipped to the postage book or given to the petty cashier.

An example of the postage book is shown below.

Date	Stamps bought	Addressee	Stamps used	Special mail	Fees from petty cash
	£ p				£ p
12 Aug	55.00	Balance b/f			
		56 1st class letters	13.44		
		23 2nd class letters	4.14		
		J Quinn Dover	49		
		L Peters York	24	Rec dely	30
		K Mitchell Detroit USA	57	Airmail	
		R Westwell Cardiff	24	Spec dely	1.95
		S Saunders Bath	2.28	parcel	
			21.40		
		Balance c/f	33.60		
	55.00		55.00		

The book is balanced either daily or weekly.

Mailroom equipment
Postage scales

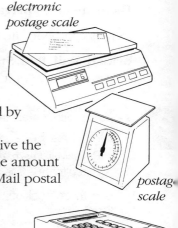

electronic postage scale

Modern postage scales are electronic. They are fitted with a special chip and when certain keys are pressed will work out the weight and rate of postage for most types of mail.

- When postage rates change, the chip has to be replaced by the manufacturer.
- Ordinary postage scales can be used but they will just give the weight of the letter or packet. You will have to check the amount of postage payable by referring to an up-to-date Royal Mail postal charges booklet.

postage scale

Franking machines

Instead of affixing postage stamps to envelopes, the machine prints the amount of postage payable on to the envelope.

- For parcels, a stick-on label is printed with the correct postage.
- For security, the machine should be locked when not in use.
- An advertising slogan of the company can be incorporated into the franked impression.

franking machine

- Franking machines are hired or purchased from manufacturers.
- A licence for a machine must be obtained from the Post Office.
- Postage units are purchased from the Post Office and set into the machine.
- A meter displays the number of units remaining in the machine. This number decreases each time the machine is used.
- When the machine is empty, more units are purchased in advance from the Post Office.
- Units can be set into later models electronically by telephoning the manufacturer for a special code to key in to the machine.
- A franking control card is completed daily to record usage. The card must be sent to the Post Office each week.

franked mail

- The date on the machine must be changed daily and more ink added when the franked impression fades.
- The amount of postage required is selected by changing dials.
- Envelopes or labels stamped in error can be saved and returned to the Post Office for credit.
- Franked mail must be put in special large envelopes marked 'Franked mail' and handed over the counter at the Post Office. It should *not* be put in an ordinary post box.

Note: Even though a company franks all of its outgoing mail, a small supply of postage stamps should be kept for emergency use.

Inserting/folding/sealing machines

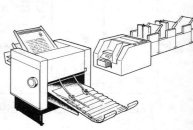

- These machines automatically fold and insert letters and enclosures into envelopes, before sealing them. Have you ever wondered how gas, electricity and telephone bills are folded and inserted so neatly into envelopes?

Section review

Complete the sentences below, using each of the following words, once only.

Parcelforce	registered
enclosures	window
jiffy	cardboard
envelope	postage
scales	internal

1 Whilst collecting the outgoing mail for despatch, the _____ mail can also be collected, ready for sorting and delivering to other departments.

2 When putting letters into envelopes for despatching by mail, care should be taken to attach all _____.

3 By using _____ envelopes, the error of putting letters into the wrong envelope is avoided.

4 The term DL refers to a size of _____.

5 The Royal Mail business now dealing with parcels is called _____.

6 To send valuable items by mail, _____ post should be used.

7 To send unbreakable items through the post, special padded packets called _____ bags can be bought from the Post Office and stationers.

8 The _____ book is used to keep a record of outgoing mail and the number of stamps used.

9 The latest postage _____ contain a chip which can calculate the amount of postage payable.

10 Fragile articles should first be wrapped securely, then packed into a stout _____ box before mailing.

WORDSEARCH

Look at the grid shown below and find the following words.

REGISTERED
MAILROOM
FREEPOST
RECORDED
DATAPOST
FRANKING
DEADLINE
SWIFTAIR
STAMP
AIRMAIL

M	A	I	L	R	O	O	M	L	D	P
D	R	E	H	J	F	D	S	I	E	M
G	V	E	N	H	G	F	R	A	A	A
N	W	Q	G	H	O	J	G	M	D	T
I	F	S	H	I	J	T	A	R	L	S
K	G	J	P	F	S	H	K	I	I	O
N	E	R	H	J	D	T	W	A	N	P
A	D	U	P	L	N	M	E	F	E	A
R	S	W	I	F	T	A	I	R	S	T
F	R	E	E	P	O	S	T	T	E	A
S	D	G	R	E	C	O	R	D	E	D

7 Reprographics

7.1 Produce copies from original documents using reprographic equipment

This section covers
- methods of reprography
  - duplicating
  - copying
- more information on photocopiers
  - functions
  - equipment problems
  - routine maintenance

    – improving quality
    – reducing wastage
- multi-page documents
- collating and fastening equipment
- returning finished work/deadlines
- copyright law
- ordering and storage of materials.

During the course of each day, many different types of documents have to be copied. This is called **reprography** – making copies.

Methods of reprography
There are a number of ways to do this.

Duplicating
Spirit copier

Used	– more in schools than offices
Quality	– not very good
Materials	– typed or handwritten master copy, liquid spirit (highly inflammable!) semi-absorbent duplicating paper
Cost	– paper, spirit and masters are reasonably cheap

spirit duplicator

Ink duplicator

Used	– in schools, colleges and organisations who need to send out newsletters/information sheets
Quality	– reasonably good
Materials	– a waxed master stencil can be typed or an original is copied onto a stencil by means of an electronic scanning machine, duplicating ink, semi-absorbent duplicating paper
Cost	– paper, ink and masters are relatively cheap, although the initial purchase of the scanning machine and ink duplicator needs to be taken into consideration. The stencils can be stored and used again.

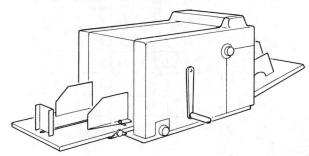

ink duplicator

Offset litho

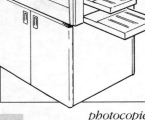

offset litho

Used — by any organisation wanting to make numerous copies

Quality — excellent and can print in more than one colour

Materials — paper or metal plates, photocopier needed to copy paper masters, solution for cleaning down machinery after use, good quality copy paper, a trained operator is needed

Cost — the actual duplicating process, for long runs, is reasonably cheap although the offset machinery is expensive to purchase and the training of an operator needs to be considered.
The stencils can be used again.

Copying

Photocopier

Used — almost everywhere! Many firms have more than one copier

Quality — excellent – sometimes better than the original document

Materials — toner ink (either in cartridge or loose powder) plain paper

Cost — most copiers are rented, charge will include engineer call out. Toner is usually included in the rental fee but paper must be provided by the user.
The user pays just over 1p per copy as well as the rental. Can prove expensive for long runs – offset would be more economical.

photocopier

Three companies rent photocopiers from separate suppliers at different rental rates.

Calculate the total photocopying cost to each company per month. (Paper is bought in packets of 500 sheets.)

Company A
Rental is £35 per month
Paper costs £5 per packet
5000 copies are made each month at a cost of 2p per copy.

Company C
Rental is £60 per month
Paper costs £3.50 per packet
15 000 copies are made each month at 1p per copy.

Company B
Rental is £50 per month
Paper costs £4 per packet
10 000 copies are made each month at 1.5p per copy.

More information on photocopiers

Functions

Photocopiers are available in a variety of sizes. The larger models could include some or all of the following functions:

- documents can be fed in automatically
- print quickly
- accept various sizes of paper
- continuous computer print-outs can be copied automatically without the need for separation

- can copy onto card, labels, offset paper plates and OHP transparencies
- adjustable density control to take account of very light or dark originals
- can enlarge or reduce, with a choice of sizes available
- will copy a document onto both sides of the paper (known as **back-to-back** or **double-sided**)
- stack multi-page documents into separate trays (to assist collating)
- operator can interrupt a job, and then resume
- an additional paper tray
- can staple multi-page documents
- book mode – will photocopy an open book without adjusting the position
- advanced machines can print in colour
- a password number can be keyed in to record the user and the number of copies being made by them. A limit can be imposed.

Check the functions available on the photocopier used in your building.

Complete as much as possible of the grid below.

If possible, obtain details of the cost involved

Function	tick ✓
Automatic paper feed	
Photocopy onto card or labels	
Reduce	
Enlarge	
Automatic back-to-back	
Prepare OHPs and offset masters	
Take paper sizes other than A4	
Automatic density adjustment	
Additional paper tray	
Interrupt facility	
Photocopy continuous computer paper	
Book mode copy facility	
Collate documents	
Staple multi-page documents	
Copy in colour (other than black)	
Rental cost per month	£
Cost of copy paper per packet	£
Additional charge per copy	p

Equipment problems

Sometimes, your photocopier will develop faults. Learn how to identify the signals from your copier. Many of these problems can be remedied by you.

The fault signals are common to most makes of machine and the instruction manual will explain these to you. On modern machines, an electronic display panel gives step-by-step instructions to remedy the fault.

Personal counter – key to operate the machine has been inserted incorrectly.

 Paper cassette is empty – needs refilling.

 Paper jam – open front cover to remove jammed paper.

 Toner required – either insert a new toner cartridge or fill with toner powder.

 Used toner container needs emptying – remove container and replace with empty container.

 Developer required – developer replacement should only be carried out by engineer.

 Collator trays need emptying – they have reached the limit which they can hold.

 Service required – call the service engineer as soon as possible.

Routine maintenance

- Keep the glass clean. Use a special spray.
- Avoid scratching the glass with paper clips or other sharp objects.
- Copiers should not be placed flat against a wall. Air should be allowed to circulate.
- Keep coffee cups and other drinks away from the copier.
- Do not poke inside the copier – send for the engineer if the fault is not easily identifiable.

Improving quality

To make sure that your finished copies are of the best possible quality

- Clean any dirty marks from the document to be copied – a special photocopy correction fluid is more suitable than liquid paper.
- Make sure the glass plate is spotless.
- Place document to be copied face down on plate (if not using automatic feed).
- Line up the document within the correct guide mark sizes – not crooked!
- Adjust the density control according to whether the document is too light or too dark. Lighten the density if you are copying from coloured paper (some copiers will do this automatically).
- Some copiers do not copy pencil or blue ink as well as black ink.
- When copying small pieces, such as newspaper cuttings, place a sheet of A4 behind your cutting.
- Do not use too much glue or Sellotape when sticking cut-outs.
- Apply *gentle* pressure to the photocopier lid when copying from thick books, to avoid light getting in.

Reducing wastage

- Check that the previous user has not left the copier set for A3, enlargement, reduction or worse still, 100 copies!
- If A5 size is required, take two copies and place both side by side on A4 paper – only half the number of copies need then be made.
- Make sure your document is placed face down – not facing upwards.
- Take the exact number of copies required – no extras 'just in case'.
- Discourage personal use of the copier by members of staff.
- When refilling the paper tray, make sure the paper is fanned to avoid multi-sheets being fed through.
- *Always* take one text copy to check before making multi-copies.
- Finally, if you are unsure of how to use any functions on your machine – *Ask* – it can prove expensive to experiment.

Multi-page documents

- Try to make sure each page is consistently numbered at either the top or the bottom of each page.
- Photocopy pages in their correct order – take extra care with back-to-back pages.
- Always straighten copies squarely by tapping them on the desk top.
- If a collator is not available on your copier, stack each set of pages offset against the previous set.

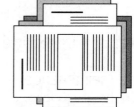

The copies are then ready for stapling or binding as required.

Stacking collated copy documents

Collating and fastening equipment

Multi-page documents can be sorted into the final order by

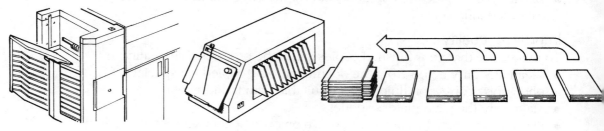

a collator attached to a photocopier *a free-standing electric collator* *sorting by hand.*

Be sure to check that the first collated pages out of a collator are in the correct order and there are none missing!

The documents can then be fastened by a number of methods.

- **Stapling** – hand or electric. A heavy duty stapler will deal with more pages.
- **Crimper** – the pages are crimped together by machine at the top corner, thus holding them together.

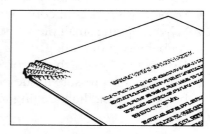

- **Hole punched** and a **treasury tag** used to hold the pages together. Alternatively, pages can be put in a ring binder.
- **Comb binder** – pages are hole punched lengthways and a plastic comb fastens pages at the spine.

- **Thermal binder** – heat fastens an adhesive spine to the pages to make a booklet.

- **Plastic side binding** – cheap and simple – a plastic strip is slid down the length of the pages to hold them together.

- Card may be used for the first and last pages to make a sturdy booklet. The outer pages can be **laminated** – a plastic covering is applied by a heat process.

- Special covers are available with cut out fronts. Title page shows through the cut out.

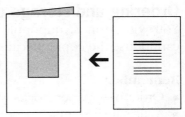

Returning finished work/deadlines

Photocopying may be requested from colleagues with specific instructions eg

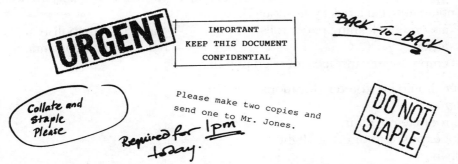

If you are unsure of any instruction, check first, before making hundreds of unwanted copies!

Always

✔ Check through all instruction requests for photocopying. Those marked urgent etc must be done first. Try to keep to deadlines – it could be important!

✔ Notify the person requesting, in a polite manner, if the request cannot be carried out – perhaps the photocopier is out of order.

✔ Complete any essential photocopying records (if your copier does not record these automatically).

✔ Finally, do check that the quality of copies is acceptable and collated documents are in the correct order – speed is no excuse for sloppy work!

'A few may have some pages missing, Mrs Pearson – but haven't I been quick!'

Copyright law

Just as you will be breaking the law if you copy a video or music tape, similarly you must not copy a published document or pages from a book, unless copyright has been waived.

You and your organisation can be prosecuted under the **Copyright, Designs and Patents Act 1988** if you do!

Schools and colleges may have permission to copy certain pages from some books – make sure you check first!

Ordering and storage of materials

You will be most unpopular if you have to notify your colleagues that they cannot use the copier because the photocopy paper has run out!

Remember

● Order new paper stocks well before current stocks are used.
● Anticipate how much paper is generally used each month and order accordingly.
● Ask colleagues to let you know well in advance of any excessive large numbers of copies being required, then you can order extra supplies.
● Keep smaller stocks of coloured paper, card, labels and OHP transparencies.
● Anticipate what stocks you should keep of
  – absorbent cleaning paper rolls   – glass cleaning polish
  – toner   – book binding consumables.
  – empty toner cartridges for used powder

Paper should be stored in locations which are
● dry
● at room temperature
● not exposed to direct sunlight
● clean.

Keep paper in the wrapper and lying flat. Unwrapped paper may become damp and curl, resulting in paper misfeeds.

Section review

Complete the sentences below, using each of the following words once only.

plain	toner
metal	fastened
trained	rental
scanner	copyright
waste	reprography

1 To photocopy pages from a book is against the _____ law.

2 Plates for offset litho duplicating can be made of paper or _____.

3 Photocopiers use _____ paper.

4 The process of reproducing documents is known as _____.

5 When copies are faint, the photocopier needs more _____.

6 An offset litho duplicator needs a _____ operator.

7 The majority of photocopiers are acquired on _____.

8 Masters for an ink duplicator can be prepared using a _____.

9 Care should be taken to keep _____ to a minimum.

10 Multi-page documents can be _____ using a variety of methods.

WORDSEARCH

Look at the grid shown below and find the following words.

DUPLICATING

COLLATE

OFFSET LITHO

THERMAL

DEADLINES

URGENT

COPYRIGHT

STAPLE

REPROGRAPHY

STENCIL

D	B	H	C	U	R	H	W	L	I	T	C
Z	O	F	F	S	E	T	L	I	T	H	O
U	R	G	E	N	T	P	T	N	S	E	P
B	S	T	A	P	L	E	L	E	P	R	Y
C	X	Y	K	S	T	J	N	F	G	M	R
J	M	V	T	A	D	I	P	C	N	A	I
X	K	T	L	K	L	F	R	K	I	L	G
F	D	L	D	D	C	L	O	G	D	L	H
B	O	M	A	F	L	Y	F	F	U	I	T
C	R	E	P	R	O	G	R	A	P	H	Y
K	D	U	P	L	I	C	A	T	I	N	G

8 Liaising with callers and colleagues

8.1 Receive and assist callers

This section covers

- types of caller
- greeting callers
- non-verbal communications
- difficult callers
- dealing with delays/non-availability
- escorting callers to destinations
- confidentiality
- security.

In section 3.2, we mentioned the importance of presenting a good company image to customers.

Can you remember how it was suggested that this image could be maintained?

If not, check back to page **54**.

Remember how important it is to attend to callers promptly and courteously.

Types of caller

Throughout each day, many callers may visit your office. They could include
- visitors with appointments
- people without appointments
- customers paying bills
- sales representatives
- new customers making enquiries about products
- people making enquiries about job vacancies
- postmen/women
- delivery persons
- people performing a service eg milkman, repairmen, telephone cleaning staff
- friends and relations of colleagues.

All these people will form an instant opinion of your company by the way and manner in which you deal with them.

Greeting callers

Look at how the receptionist dealt with the *seven* callers below, then write down how you would have responded to each caller.

- **Person enquiring about a job vacancy**
'We have some application forms somewhere but I just can't find them. Can you call back tomorrow?'

- **New customer**
'Yes, what do you want?'

- **Photocopier engineer**
'I hope your van isn't blocking anybody in on the car park. You won't be too popular!'

- **Customer paying a bill of £20.10 with three £10 notes**
  'You're going to take all our small change!'

- **Visitor with appointment**
  'You'll have to wait. Mr Fairhurst is still dictating some letters to his secretary.'

- **Sales representative**
  'We have a very strict rule which I am not allowed to break. Sales reps are only seen on Wednesdays and Fridays by appointment.'

- **Customer enquiring about a product**
  'I don't really know much about this item. I haven't a clue how it works.'

Discuss with your tutor and the other members of your group how you would have responded.

Non-verbal communications

Remember, callers do not necessarily have to communicate verbally with you in order to transmit information. The way they look at you, move, and the expressions on their faces can let you know what they are thinking or feeling.

The actions of *four* different callers are described below. Match each one against the descriptions shown in the end column.

1 Reluctant to approach the desk, looks round continually.　　**A** *angry*

2 Taps on the desk for your attention whilst you are dealing with another caller.　　**B** *pleasant*

3 Glares at you whilst waiting for attention.　　**C** *nervous*

4 Smiles warmly at you whilst approaching the desk.　　**D** *impatient*

Have you decided which description matches the actions of each of the four callers?

These signals are called **non-verbal communications**. They tell you a lot about callers before you actually speak to them. You must learn how to interpret these signals. And remember – the signals you give out will tell callers a lot about you !

Difficult callers

Angry, aggressive caller
- Be polite and patient.
- Listen without interrupting.
- Get help if you cannot deal with the situation yourself.

Shy, nervous caller
- Try to put them at ease with a friendly smile.
- Listen carefully to what they have to say.
- Give any information slowly and quietly – repeating it for them if necessary.

Callers without appointments

- Use your common sense here. If you think there is a possibility of the caller being seen, discreetly make enquiries.
- Otherwise, offer to make an appointment.
- For persistent reps, ask them to make an appointment or take their business card to pass on.

Callers making collections

- Check what the policy of your company is about making donations. They can become a nuisance.

People who want to stay and chat

- Often they are friends or relatives waiting for one of your colleagues.
- Try to discourage them from taking up too much of your time.
- Offer them a seat away from your desk, direct them to the washroom, give them a magazine.
- If all this fails – politely say how you would love to chat but you have too much work to do!

Dealing with delays/non-availability

If there is a delay in callers being attended to

- If possible, explain the reason for the delay.
- Ask them to sit down – do not leave them standing.
- Offer tea/coffee or a magazine.
- Direct them to the washroom, if required.
- Reassure them regularly that they have not been forgotten.
- After ten minutes, remind the member of staff that the caller is still waiting.
- Try to make occasional conversation with them, without interrupting your work routine – 'Have you travelled far?'
- When they can eventually be seen, be sure to apologise for the delay.

If it is not possible for the caller to be dealt with

- Explain the reason fully eg, 'Mr Watts is away in London until tomorrow.'
- See if anyone else could deal with the matter.
- Offer to pass on a message, provide a notepad and pen, if required.
- Make an appointment for a later date.
- Pass a message to the member of staff concerned informing them of the caller's visit.

Escorting callers to destinations

Moving visitors from reception to another part of the building will depend upon the procedure operated by the company.

Callers may

- be given directions to the place of their appointment
- be collected by the person they have come to see or by a secretary
- be escorted by a member of the office or security staff.

Whilst escorting visitors, make polite conversation with them, open doors for them and point out any hazards to be avoided. Introduce visitors to the person they have called to see, if they are not already known.

General rules for introductions are

- Introduce a man to a woman.
  'Miss Armstrong, this is Mr Parker, our Sales Manager.'
- Introduce a younger woman to an older one.
- Introduce a younger man to an older one.
- When introducing a husband and wife, mention them both.
  'Mr Blake, this is Mr and Mrs Wilton. Mr and Mrs Wilton, this is Mr Blake, our Accountant.'
- When introducing a visitor to a group of people, introduce the individual first.
  'Mrs Clarkson, this is Mr Baker, Mr Kent and Mr Slater. Gentlemen, meet Mrs Clarkson.'

Confidentiality

If one of your duties is to attend to callers, follow these guidelines.

- *Never* disclose any confidential information about the company or the staff who work there. If you are unsure about what you may disclose, *ask* someone more senior!
- *Do not* discuss personal or financial matters with callers when other visitors can listen. Offer some degree of privacy.
- Take care when speaking on the telephone in a reception area. *Make sure* visitors do not overhear private information.

Finally, do not gossip!

Security

For larger companies, security begins in the car park. Security guards will record car registration numbers and issue badges to visitors. Different coloured badges may indicate access only to specified areas.

Further checks should be made on casual callers.

Callers may be asked to leave baggage with the guards to be collected on departure.

Visitors are often asked to complete and sign a **Visitors' register** or **Callers' log** giving their name, company and details of their visit.

VISITORS' REGISTER						
Date 12 May 199–						
Time	Caller's name	Company	Car Reg No	Called to see	Business	Time of departure
0900	John Dean	Brightwell Industries	J413TKY	Peter Kay	Advertising contact	1015
0915	Susan Kent	–	–	Jean Bond	Job interview	1000
1020	L Seymour	Seymour Commercials	H318LBX	G Pointer	Transport	1115

The visitor's badge will be handed back when departing.

Because of recent incidents of explosives being found in public places, many companies do not allow callers to move out of the reception area. Members of staff will come down to reception to conduct any business there.

Generally, a number of interview rooms are available. This eliminates the need for callers to wander around the building unescorted.

All staff should
- close and lock all windows after use
- keep offices locked when not occupied
- never leave handbags or jackets on desks and chairs unattended – lock them away out of sight
- never leave cash on desks unattended
- lock office doors when counting money eg wages, banking
- keep a look-out for unattended bags or parcels left on the premises
- challenge any unauthorised person seen on the premises (particularly if acting suspiciously).

Section review

Use the following words, once only, to complete the sentences below.

confidential	register
delay	introducing
security	greeting
difficult	image
appointments	escort

1 A suitable _____ to visitors would be 'Good morning, can I help you?'

2 If there is a _____ in a member of staff keeping an appointment, the visitor could be offered refreshments.

3 An efficient receptionist should give a good _____ of the company.

4 Certain courtesy rules should be followed when _____ visitors to the person they have come to see.

5 As a _____ measure, a note is often made of visitors' car registration numbers.

6 It is advisable to _____ callers from reception to the person they have called to see.

7 Tact should be used when dealing with _____ callers.

8 Sales representatives should be encouraged to make _____ rather than just call hoping to see the Sales Manager.

9 When speaking on the telephone, in the presence of visitors, you must take care not to disclose _____ matters.

10 In many companies, visitors are asked to sign a _____.

Crossword

Across

1 The receptionist should create a good .... of the company (5)
2 Be on the lookout for these left unattended (4)
4 Rooms not occupied should be kept .... (6)
6 Callers should be greeted in a .... manner (6)
7 A caller (7)
8 Sales reps should be encouraged to make one of these (11)

Down

2 An item which visitors may be requested to wear (5)
3 Without speaking, signals given by callers (3) (6)
5 Provided by employing guards (8)
6 The attention all visitors should receive (6)

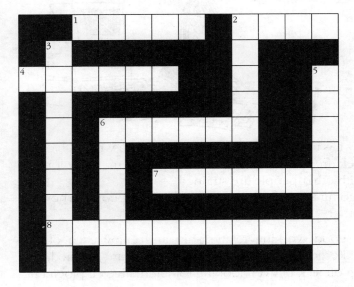

8.2 Maintain business relationships with other members of staff

This section covers

- working with business colleagues
- difficulties in working relationships
- communicating with senior staff
- organising the workload
- importance of dress, appearance and behaviour.

Working with business colleagues

Be honest!

Do you get on with every person you work with or everybody in your class?

Probably very few people can answer 'yes'.

'I can't help Joanna check these figures, Mrs Pearson, 'cos I'm not speaking to her this week!'

There are two reasons why it is important for employees to get on with each other.

- At least 36 hours a week are spent at work and this can seem a very long time if relationships with other people are strained.
- Your employer is not going to get 100 per cent effort from people who cannot work well together.

Employees who have a good working relationship and enjoy each other's company will generally like going to work. When relations are strained, this can lead to people staying off sick or even looking for alternative employment.

Difficulties in working relationships

Difficulties can arise in many ways and it is important to recognise how these can occur. Reasons could include:

- one person not pulling their weight – continually trying to avoid jobs
- not being willing to work as part of a team
- continually producing inaccurate, sloppy work
- unnecessarily trying to gain favour with senior staff
- not bothering to take or pass on messages to colleagues
- continually arriving late and wanting to leave early
- taking excessive sick leave
- discussing one colleague with another
- staff competing with one another for promotion
- not sharing *all* jobs eg tea-making, washing cups, errands
- starting, and passing on, malicious gossip.

Can you honestly say that none of the above reasons applies to you!

Remember, you don't necessarily have to like colleagues – just get on with them!

If you are ever in the wrong, have the courage to admit it and apologise. It will prevent a lot of unpleasantness.

Communicating with senior staff

There is nothing more embarrassing for an employer or supervisor than an employee being over-familiar!

When starting a new job, you should try to assess how senior staff will expect you to behave towards them.

Tips to follow

- Watch how other staff on your level relate to people in authority.
- Address seniors with a title eg 'Mr Parkinson', 'Mrs Bennett' until you are invited to use their first name.
- Politely respond to general conversation without becoming too chatty.
- *Never* ask personal questions, 'What does your wife think about this?', 'How much did that cost you?'
- Be discreet. Never gossip about anything which is said to you in confidence.
- Avoid running down colleagues and tale-telling to senior staff. The consequences of this could be quite serious – for you!

Organising the workload

Assume that you have arrived at your workplace – an insurance office – just before 9 am. Your job involves general clerical duties, including some telephone work and dealing with occasional callers.

Look at the list of jobs below which are waiting for your attention. Write down the order in which you feel you should deal with these jobs.

1 *Paul Shannon has given you 2 pages of figures to be checked by calculator. He wants them before 2pm today.*

2 30 page document needs photocopying and binding – before the end of next week.

3 Filing away documents and copy letters from yesterday

4 Your manager, Simon Watson, wants two files for Paul Heaton who has an appointment with him at 10am today.

5 *The photocopier broke down at 5.30 last night. The engineer needs to be called out by telephone – urgent!*

6 A cheque is to be made out for £284.60 payable to James Pearson, who will collect it at 9.30 this morning. Mr Watson will sign the cheque.

7 Mr Watson has asked you to telephone Acorn Garage to inform them that he will be about half an hour late for his 11 am appointment this morning.

8 *Buy new batteries for the spare calculator – they were needed two weeks ago!*

9 *Make out a cheque to pay the office gas bill at the end of the month.*

10 Two letters want typing for Susan Patterson. She is leaving for London in one hour but has said you can sign the letters on her behalf before posting them.

11 Telephone British Rail for Mr Watson to find the train times to London and return for his visit on Friday of next week.

12 *Telephone Mrs Pamela Kent with some quotation figures for which she telephoned yesterday. – before 9.30 am.*

13 Three letters to be typed for Michael Kenyon. He will sign the letters before he leaves the office at noon.

14 Type the Assessor's Report for Michael Kenyon for next month's meeting.

Discuss with your tutor, the order in which you will deal with these jobs. Give reasons for your choice of order.

Importance of dress, appearance and behaviour

Jill and Paul both work in the same estate agency in the town centre. They deal with prospective house purchasers and other business callers and are aware of the need to maintain a good image of the agency.

Look at the two illustrations below. Can you recognise Jill and Paul?

Did you choose the illustration on the right? Actually, both pictures are of Jill and Paul. The illustration on the left shows them ready for a night at the local disco!

Jill and Paul are sensible enough to realise that there is one way of dressing for work and a totally different way of dressing for a night out!

Many firms now encourage staff to wear a uniform and this eliminates the problem of maintaining standards of dress.

Your employer has a right to expect from you
- an acceptable standard of dress
- care to be taken with your appearance – tidy hairstyle, clean nails (not bitten!) and clean shoes
- Polite, well-mannered behaviour.

Remember, the image of a company is very dependent upon its employees.

Section review

Fill in the missing letters and then write the completed words in your folder to help you remember them.

1 Requests from colleagues should be responded to w_ll__g_y.

2 Work should be planned so that d__dl_n_s can be kept to.

3 An employer has a right to expect a well-groomed _pp__r_nc_ of an employee.

4 It is important to be able to c___un_c_te with senior staff.

5 You must organise your w___lo_d at the beginning of each day.

6 It is important for co__eag__s to work well together.

7 Many companies now ask staff to wear a _n_f_rm to present a good image of the company.

8 Staff who are in the wrong should have the courage to ap___gis_.

9 When addressing senior staff for the first time, you should use a courtesy t___e.

10 Hair, nails and shoes should always be c___n.

WORDSEARCH

Look at the grid shown below and find the following words.

CLEAN

CALLERS

WORKLOAD

DRESS

COLLEAGUE

IMAGE

DISCREET

POLITE

STANDARDS

BEHAVIOUR

H	C	O	L	L	E	A	G	U	E	Y
S	F	G	U	G	K	P	A	D	T	N
G	C	E	A	T	P	O	U	R	T	R
C	X	M	P	U	O	T	U	E	E	C
G	I	B	F	D	L	O	R	S	E	A
G	U	O	G	H	I	K	O	S	R	L
F	S	H	T	V	T	U	R	F	C	L
C	L	E	A	N	E	B	V	H	S	E
F	E	H	T	G	H	R	E	W	I	R
K	E	S	T	A	N	D	A	R	D	S
B	K	U	W	O	R	K	L	O	A	D

9 Health and safety

9.1 Operate safely in the workplace

This section covers

- recognising danger at work
- safety procedures to follow
- fire fighting equipment
- the law on health and safety
- safe working practices
- accidents at work.

Recognising danger at work

Look at the pictures below. Each one illustrates *two* possible dangerous situations. Can you identify them?

Dangerous situations such as these are often referred to as **potential hazards**.

It is your duty to recognise potential hazards and, if you cannot deal with them yourself, you must report the danger to your supervisor or the person who has been appointed to look after safety matters in your building. This person is called the **safety representative**.

Make a list of any additional potential hazards which may occur in your school, college or workplace.

Compare your list with those of other members of your group and discuss with your tutor how these situations can be avoided.

Safety procedures to follow

It is usual nowadays for all new employees to go through a period of **induction** when beginning a new job. This means being introduced to colleagues, the duties they will be expected to carry out, how the Company operates (known as **working practices**), and familiarisation with the building and factory.

During the tour of the building, the new employee should be made aware of the following:

- layout of the building
- all entrances and exits (including emergency exits)
- location of fire alarms and how to operate these
- location and type of fire fighting equipment
  - eg   fire extinguishers
      fire blankets
      buckets of sand

- procedure for leaving (**evacuating**) the building in an emergency
- the assembly point
- method of checking that all employees and visitors have left the building.

Can you think of any other reasons, apart from fire, why a building would have to be evacuated quickly?

Fire fighting equipment

There are different types of fire extinguishers, each containing either water or a chemical suitable for dealing with a fire. Most fires falls into two main classes.

- **Class A:** wood, cloth, paper, plastics, coal etc
- **Class B:** grease, fats, oil, paint, petrol etc.

To enable people to recognise which extinguisher to use for putting out different types of fire, extinguishers are made in varied shapes and colours.

Fire blankets are made of special material and used for smothering flames eg chip pan fires. It is advisable to keep these blankets in a kitchen or other cooking area in case of fire.

Your tutor will give you a sheet illustrating *seven* different types of fire extinguisher (page 156). Note which extinguisher should be used to put out the different types of fire.

Look around your school, college or workplace (or other public building) and see if you can recognise any of these extinguishers.

Discuss with your tutor the different colours used for these extinguishers, then colour in the illustrations on the sheet with the correct colour. Keep this sheet in your folder for reference.

The law on health and safety

In 1974, the Government passed the **Health and Safety at Work Act** (known as **HASAWA 1974**). This states that **both** employer and employee must accept responsibility for health and safety in the workplace.

The **employer** must provide
- a safe entrance and exit from work
- safe working conditions
- safe methods of operating machinery and equipment
- proper arrangements for handling, storing and using dangerous liquids and substances
- training and adequate supervision and instruction for all employees
- an enquiry into all accidents.

The **employee** must
- take reasonable care for his or her *own* health and safety
- take reasonable care for the health and safety of *other* people
- cooperate with the employer or any other person appointed to carry out duties under the Act.

Safe working practices

Employees should be encouraged to work safely.

Use of equipment
- Follow manufacturer's instructions.
- Check for trailing leads, broken sockets and frayed wires.
- Make sure that rings and trailing jewellery do not interfere with operating equipment.
- Arrange for proper ventilation when using equipment which gives of dangerous fumes eg photocopiers.
- Avoid leaving drawers of filing cabinets open.

Furniture

- Use adjustable chairs when operating keyboard equipment, to prevent backache.
- Use safety step ladders or safety stools when reaching items from high shelves.

New technology

- Avoid operating VDU equipment for long periods without a break (can cause headaches and eyestrain).
- Eliminate glare on VDU screens by using sunblinds.
- Working surfaces should be correct height for either writing or keyboarding.

Good housekeeping

- Keep the working area tidy and clean.
- Store dangerous or inflammable liquids and substances in a safe, well-ventilated place in clearly labelled containers (**Note:** – thinners and ammonia need to be used in some copying processes).

Accommodation

- Offices can be closed or open plan. This means either a series of separate rooms or staff located in one large room separated by screens. Staff should not be overcrowded.
- Windows in direct sunlight should be fitted with blinds or curtains and there should be suitable lighting.
- Floor surfaces should be neither slippery nor worn.
- Toilets should be clean with hand-washing facilities.
- It is of benefit to staff if decorating is carried out on a regular basis.

Noise

- Keep to a minimum where possible eg special covers (known as **acoustic hoods**) can be placed on noisy printers.

Safe working habits

- Do not lift objects which are too heavy but, if unavoidable, bend knees, keeping back straight and take the strain in your legs – not your back.

Temperature

- Should be above 61°F (16°C) but not too hot.
- There should be adequate ventilation.

Accidents at work

Most accidents at work can be avoided. Many are the result of carelessness and include

- trapping and cutting fingers
- walking into doors
- falling down steps
- lifting heavy objects
- insect stings or bites
- minor electric shocks.

Larger companies may have a nurse but most organisations have a list of qualified **first aiders** who can give first aid assistance.

Although many organisations do not have a sick room, all works and offices should have a **first aid box**. Drugs are *never* kept in first aid boxes and should not be offered to people who are feeling unwell.

Check the contents of the first aid box in your organisation. Make a list of the items and discuss the contents with your tutor.

Details of all accidents should be recorded in an **accident book**.

Typical entries would look like this.

Date	Time	Name of injured person	How did accident happen	Details of injury and treatment given	Name of witness	Was accident report form completed? Yes/No
6 May	9.30	Clare Taylor	Trapped hand in door	Hand swollen – taken to hosp.	Ken Page	Yes
9 May	2.00	Jason Kent	Cut finger opening package	Small cut – plaster applied	Sue Lund	No

Depending on the policy of the organisation, often an **accident report form** is also completed. This form is filed away and may need to be referred to if the injured person makes a claim against the company in respect of the injuries sustained.

Your tutor will give you a blank accident report form (page 157). Read through all the questions on this form before looking at the details of an accident given below. When you have familiarised yourself with these details, complete the accident report form, paying particular attention to accuracy and neatness.

Accident details

Matthew Kingston, aged 28, from the Accounts Department, slipped down the stairs whilst leaving the canteen. He grazed his back quite badly and dislocated his thumb whilst trying to save himself. He was taken to the first aid room by Simon Walker, who was with him at the time of the accident, but it was decided to take him to hospital for an X-ray on his thumb. His arm was put in a sling to ease the pain.

The accident happened today at 1.15 pm. Matthew's home address is 15 Tenby Close, Bridgetown.

After completing the form, you should sign this as the person reporting the accident and date with today's date.

Section review

Fill in the missing letters and then write the completed words in your folder to help you remember what they mean.

1 _x__ngui_h__s are supplied in different sizes and colours and contain special liquids for fighting fires.

2 The Health and Safety at Work Act 1974 is often referred to in the abbreviated form of H___WA.

3 Possible dangerous situations are referred to as p__ent___ __zard_.

4 When a person is injured at work, a record should be made in the _ccid__t _oo_.

5 Care should always be taken when operating __ch__ery.

6 When the fire alarm is sounded, everyone should _v_c__te the building.

7 Plasters, bandages and scissors are some of the items which are kept in the f___t __d __x.

8 Buildings are evacuated in the event of fires or b__b th___ts.

9 In offices, the ___perat___ should be at least 61°F (16°C) after the first hour.

10 The person appointed to look after safety in your building is called the s___ty __pr__ent___ve.

WORDSEARCH

Look at the grid shown below and find the following words.

HAZARDS

ACCIDENT

SAFETY

RULES

AUTHORITY

DANGEROUS

ACT

POLICY

FIRE

ALARM

Y	F	S	S	J	V	H	B	K	G	S	W
S	T	L	U	S	W	T	C	P	U	T	N
L	N	I	O	P	O	L	I	C	Y	R	Q
O	E	F	R	A	L	A	R	M	S	U	M
J	D	B	E	O	E	V	K	D	D	L	V
X	I	N	G	K	H	S	F	I	R	E	P
H	C	W	N	Y	E	T	E	G	A	S	I
N	C	H	A	U	M	C	U	O	Z	T	M
Q	A	V	D	J	M	P	J	A	A	C	T
D	F	V	F	P	Q	A	L	U	H	L	C
F	W	G	C	M	O	Q	J	L	Q	Z	M
J	L	P	E	U	X	S	A	F	E	T	Y

10 Applying for a job

Towards the end of your training, you will be thinking about applying for a job.

By now you will probably have formed a definite idea of the type of work you would like to do.

Generally, the larger the organisation, the more specialised the work, eg

copy typist
word processing operator
data processing clerk
filing clerk
receptionist

A smaller office may offer the opportunity of more varied duties which may include all of the following:

answering the telephone
dealing with callers
handling the mail
some filing, reprography, typing or word processing

Look for vacancies in your local newspaper, the career's office or a job centre. Perhaps your college or training agency receives details of vacancies.

Prepare a **curriculum vitae (CV)** of your achievements. Ask your tutor to check through your draft for spelling mistakes or to see if you have left anything out.

Use a word processor then the CV can be updated, eg when examination results are received.

You may like to use the layout on the following page.

Do check that people are willing to let you use their name as a referee. They could include

College tutors
Present or previous employers (including a part-time job)
Secondary school year head
Supervisor of any voluntary work undertaken by you
A long standing friend of the family holding a position of responsibility

CURRICULUM VITAE

NAME:

ADDRESS:

TELEPHONE:

DATE OF BIRTH:

EDUCATION:

QUALIFICATIONS:

RESULTS AWAITED:

WORK EXPERIENCE:

REFERENCES:

INTERESTS:

A short, neat, handwritten or typed letter should accompany your CV.

---

17 Temple Gardens
Bridgetown
BR2 3GK

6 May 199 -

The Manager
BKR Manufacturing Company
27–31 Taylor Street
BRIDGETOWN
BR1 7KZ

Dear Sir

I would like to be considered for the position of clerk/typist
which was advertised in the Bridgetown Evening News.

My one-year secretarial course at Bridgetown College
finishes at the end of the month and I enclose a copy of
my CV showing what I hope to achieve.

I look forward to hearing from you in due course.

Yours faithfully

Julie Prescott

Use good quality paper (*never* a page torn from an exercise book).

Buy a pack of matching DL white envelopes and use the minimum number of
folds for your letter and CV. This will create a good first impression with the
person receiving your application.

Draft out your CV, using the example on the previous page. Ask your tutor to check
it before preparing and printing it on a word processor.

Write out or type a letter to accompany your CV applying for the following vacancy.

RECEPTIONIST
Aged 16 +. Must have excellent telephone manner,
knowledge of computers and word processing.

Hours 9 am – 5.15 pm, half hour lunch. Wage
negotiable. Please send C.V. to:

Ms Jackie Nixon,
Groupe Panache Units 10/11
Daisy Hill Ind. Est.
Ashworth Street
BRIDGETOWN
BR3 6QT

---

11 The interview

Preparation

- Find out all you can about the organisation. Interviewers will always be impressed by candidates who have done their homework and it will enable you to ask relevant questions during the interview.

- Find out where the organisation is located and decide how you will get to the interview. Check out bus or train timetables beforehand.

- The organisation may have sent you an application form to complete prior to the interview. Take a photocopy to enable you to draft out your answers before completing the form neatly.

- Decide before the actual day what you will wear to the interview and make sure the outfit is clean and pressed. Do not leave this job until a few hours before!

  Choose an outfit in which you feel smart and comfortable – perhaps a suit or a jacket and skirt. Avoid micro skirts and jeans.

  Check that hair, nails and shoes are clean.

- Think about the possible questions you may have to answer and plan your answers <u>now</u>!

  – What subjects were included in your training course?
  – What made you apply for this position?
  – Why are you seeking new employment?
  – Tell me about yourself.

Do not leave any of these things until the morning of the interview!

On the day

- Avoid arriving late at all costs. (Remember your preparation.)

- When meeting your interviewer, shake hands firmly.

- Take a seat only when invited to do so.

- Put your case/handbag by the side of your chair (don't forget it when you leave).

- Look at the interviewer in the eye when you talk.

- Avoid smoking, even if invited to do so.

- Be prepared to enlarge on your answers. Never reply just 'Yes' or 'No'.

- Remember to speak clearly and do not mumble. Avoid slang expressions and try to use correct grammar. Keep ... er and ... um to an absolute minimum.

- Do not mention personal details

  eg problems at home
  boyfriends/girlfriends.

- The interviewer wil not be impressed with answers such as

  'I find my present job boring'
  'I am after more money'.

A more positive response would be

  'I enjoy my present job but I feel ready to take on more responsibility'

- At the end of the interview, you will probably be asked if there is anything further you wish to know. You could ask

  'Will there be the possibility of day release to further my studies?'
  'What opportunities are there for promotion?'

If there is nothing you wish to ask, you could conclude the interview by saying

  'I think you have covered all aspects of the position fully and I look forward to hearing from you.'

With a colleague, practise asking and answering questions. These needn't be just work-related – any practice in speaking clearly and putting together answers is good for you. It will help you to think on your feet.

Key to activities

1.1 File documents and open new files within an established filing system

Page 5 – documents for filing

letters received

copy letters

memos

orders

quotations

delivery notes

invoices

statements

receipts

insurance documents

legal documents

Page 6 – alphabetical order

Adams, R & Co Ltd

Adamson, Paul

Black, R

Black, Robert

Bread Shop, The

Clark, Pauline

Clarke, Peter

Environment, Department of the

Green, Trevor

Greengate Hotel

McIvor, Julian

St Thomas' Nursery

Samuel, Charles

7-day Service Company

VDU Sales Ltd

Vintage Wine Company

Page 7 – numerical order

731 – P Bentley

7249 – S Belling

7543 – D Botham

7621 – L Boston

73814 – D Burgess

74256 – K Berry

74723 – A Barker

75231 – W Battersby

76241 – R Bodworth

77472 – T Barton

77571 – R Bottomly

77593 – M Bickley

Page 9 – index cards

Name	FOSTER, STEPHEN	Number	3742
Address	27 CANTERBURY WAY BRISTOL BS98 4RG		
Telephone No 0272 576684		Date of birth	27-12-55
Details			

Name	DIXON, PAULINE	Number	2895
Address	49 PRINGLE DRIVE DUNFERMLINE KY45 9KJ		
Telephone No 0383 463532		Date of birth	12-06-71
Details			

Name	SHAIKH, HANIF	Number	2832
Address	48 PORTLAND STREET LEICESTER LE2 7DD		
Telephone No 0533 564739		Date of birth	14-9-60
Details			

Name	O'DRISCOLL, JOHN	Number	3275
Address	312 DEVONPORT ROAD PRESTON PR5 2FG		
Telephone No 0772 465832		Date of birth	08-08-65
Details			

Page 11 – microfiche readers
reference libraries
banks
building societies

Page 12 – section review

1	vertical cabinet	6	suspension filing
2	wallet folder	7	punch
3	card index box	8	ring binder
4	file labels	9	stapler
5	box file	10	filing stool

Page 12
(*order of missing words*)

release	vertical
sorted	suspended
alphabetical	cross reference
numerical	confidential
index	microfiche

1.2 Identify and retrieve documents from within an established filing system

Page 13 – index card details
Full name
Address (including post code)
Date of birth
Telephone number
Reference number

Other information could include a credit limit. Personal details (such as telephone number) can be obtained from the index card, thus avoiding the need to borrow the file.

Page 14 – absent card

OUT

FILE BORROWED	BORROWER'S NAME	DEPARTMENT	DATE BORROWED	DATE RETURNED
CONTROL SERVICES PLC	Jane Mortimer	Accounts	3 February	5 February
HAMILTON & CO	Fatima Sidal	Purchasing	7 February	7 February
KEY BUSINESS SYSTEMS	Julie Carter	Technical	9 February	13 February
MEHMOOD KHAN	Gary Rogers	Personnel	15 February	16 February
STAR ENGINEERING PLC	Tony Wilkins	Sales	21 February	

Page 15 – explanation for missing file

Points to include:

- Explain immediately why file is not available.
- Use a polite, informative manner.
- Give name of the person who is currently using the file and how long the file has been absent.
- State what action you will be taking to retrieve the file.

Action to take

You could request the filing clerk to chase up the file from Simon Boston

or ask Simon Boston yourself if he has finished using the file

or ask if he would be prepared to let Mr Kingsley borrow the file after which you will return it to him.

Page 16 – section review

1 alignment
2 alphabetical
3 wallet, manilla
4 suspension
5 cross reference

6 confidential
7 departmental
8 out, absent
9 reminder
10 safety

Page 16 – crossword

2.1 Process incoming and outgoing business telephone calls

Page 21 – telephone numbers and codes

1–8 no key possible
9   010 353 1
10   010 34 22

11 010 39 6
12 010 49 89

Page 25 – section review

1 secrecy
2 peak
3 VDU
4 TouchTone
5 cheap

6 answering
7 message
8 extensions
9 reference
10 freefone

Page 25 – wordsearch

R	B	O	P	E	R	A	T	O	R	S
D	I	R	E	C	T	O	R	Y	E	Y
J	N	S	G	H	J	I	Y	G	E	C
C	T	R	H	E	J	K	A	Y	S	N
H	E	S	W	A	Z	P	X	N	T	E
A	R	D	G	P	W	F	H	G	A	G
R	N	G	T	O	E	A	W	S	N	R
G	A	L	L	P	I	U	T	E	D	E
E	L	L	A	S	X	L	C	Q	A	M
S	E	C	U	R	I	T	Y	Y	R	E
Y	S	E	Q	S	D	S	G	Y	D	T

2.2 Receive and relay oral and written messages

Page 27 – incorrect messages

7 March   – no date given
8 March   – no telephone number for daughter's house
9 March   – only 3 reps names given
10 March – time message received is omitted
11 March – total of £120 is incorrect, should be £110
12 March – message too brief – not clear

Page 29 – section review

1 extension
2 alphabet
3 day
4 question
5 urgent

6 pen, pencil
7 verbal
8 neatly
9 name
10 time

2.3 Supply information for a specific purpose

Page 32 – where to find information

1 AA handbook, travel agent
2 Travel agent, bank, newspaper
3 Travel agent, teletext
4 *Who's Who*
5 Dictionary
6 Mileage distance chart in a diary, road atlas or AA handbook
7 Newspaper, *Radio Times* or teletext
8 Newspaper, teletext
9 Post Office Counters Ltd
10 Parcelforce

Page 34 – section review

1	dictionary	**6**	oral
2	directory	**7**	index
3	viewdata	**8**	deadline
4	microfiche	**9**	newspaper
5	colleagues	**10**	graph

1	subject to change	**6**	subject to change
2	071	**7**	Valletta
3	Solent	**8**	subject to change
4	Member of the European Parliament	**9**	Roberts
5	subject to change	**10**	*Curriculum vitae*

2.4 Draft routine business communications
Page 36 – grammar

1	were	**4**	anywhere
2	taught	**5**	taller
3	is	**6**	are

Page 39 – Homonyms
1 a wear **b** were **c** where
2 a there **b** their
3 a too **b** two **c** to
4 a has **b** as
5 a fare **b** fair
6 a off **b** of
7 a know **b** no
8 a cheque **b** check

Page 41– apostrophe
1 Isn't
2 you'll John's
3 There's Jack's
4 We'll manager's o'clock
5 can't it's

Page 41– vocabulary, alternative words
1 exact, copy, same
2 double meaning, doubtful, uncertain
3 rouse, incite, annoy, cause, irritate
4 share, take part, join in
5 support, prove

Page 46 – section review

1	hyphen	**6**	vocabulary
2	dictionary	**7**	short
3	memo	**8**	colon
4	complimentary	**9**	style
5	apostrophe	**10**	spelling

Page 46 – wordsearch

C	R	W	S	P	E	L	L	I	N	G	D
S	O	D	F	V	X	X	F	Y	R	E	P
A	E	N	Q	U	I	R	Y	C	S	H	U
Q	L	V	F	B	R	Y	H	P	W	S	N
H	A	E	B	I	W	P	V	R	K	A	C
D	Y	C	B	W	R	K	Y	E	W	D	T
B	O	N	G	R	A	M	M	A	R	W	U
P	U	E	D	F	H	J	A	D	W	U	A
V	T	T	J	H	L	E	T	T	E	R	T
S	X	N	K	L	Q	S	T	P	I	W	I
D	B	E	K	R	E	T	Y	H	J	O	O
S	W	S	A	L	U	T	A	T	I	O	N

3.1 Produce alpha/numerical information in typewritten form

Page 47 – jobs involving keyboards

secretary
typist
word processing operator
data processing operator
accounts clerk
computer programmer
travel clerk
telesales on newspapers

mail order telephonist
credit card customer services
bank clerk
building society cashier
insurance clerk
receptionist
etc.

Page 52 – section review

a First paragraph – there (not their)
b Monday (needs initial capital)
Larnaca (not 'Lanaca')
our (not 'are control')
rescheduled (not 'resheduled')
their (not 'there wish')

Page 53 – wordsearch

T	F	F	J	Z	W	I	R	M	Z	Y	K
C	S	X	P	R	I	N	T	E	R	C	C
E	J	T	K	E	Y	B	O	A	R	D	E
R	L	E	U	M	X	A	N	H	G	L	H
R	A	E	S	A	C	O	U	S	T	I	C
O	P	U	C	F	I	S	Q	D	U	M	L
C	A	Z	G	T	J	G	U	K	O	L	L
R	W	D	C	C	R	X	G	H	Y	L	E
F	D	I	A	V	G	O	C	L	A	K	P
V	D	U	Y	D	R	B	N	G	L	G	S
F	H	R	T	E	C	H	N	I	Q	U	E
S	Q	S	G	J	O	L	M	T	C	R	S

3.2 Identify and mark errors on scripted material, for correction

Page 54 – identifying errors

1 committee   week's
2 separate   mail. (not?)
3 catalogues   companies. (insert full stop)
4 accommodation   Venice, (insert comma)
5 occasions   jeans? (not full stop)

Page 55 – proof-reading skills

1 Michael was looking forward to his first day at Collage has he knew the
  qual-ifications which he had achieved would help him to progress atwork.
2 If most ofyour money is in a building society, A fall of intrest rates can only
  mean a drop on your standard of living
3 Most children watch television for atleast four hours each day? It as been
  sugested that this is the reason for the fall in reading standard.
4 The heaviest snowfall usually occurs in Febuary allthough heavy fall have
  been known to occur in march. I can remember a particularly bad year
  when i was a child.

Page 55 – checking by calculator

1 incorrect – should be £232.65
2 correct
3 correct
4 incorrect – balance owing is £188
5 incorrect – discount should be £37.50

Page 56 letter incorporating correction signs

```
13 September 199_

Mrs Clare Hindle
516 Parkhurst Lane
GLASGOW
G71 0XD

Dear Madam

We are unable to supply the pattern which you ordered because
it is temporarily out of stock.  We enclose a replacement
label for the one which you have used and would suggest you
re-order the correct pattern from our latest catalogue.

The cost of your replacement pattern should not exceed the
price originally paid.  Please return your order to us, using
the enclosed pre-paid envelope.

Yours faithfully



P Mason
Director


Enc
```

CRUISING

Have you ever considered a cruise for your anual holiday

There is a magnificent choice available with prices ranging from a very modest £495 to 9995.

Pampered passengers has the choice of superb cuisine, five resturants, four swimming pools three lounge bars, a theater, two ballrooms, a disco and a casino.

Such a choice of things todo means that every passenger can can enjoy the lifestyle which suits him or her best. You day could drift lazily past with a quite stroll on deck, a game of bridge, a piano recital or a lecture from a well-known personality

uc on the otherhand, you may prefer to tone up in the health

lc spa, swing golf club, take in a show and then dance under the stars until another day dawns.

There are big savings for children, as well as for three or four adults sharing a room and to have an extra week can cost as little as £50 per person.

uc Jamaca, the Bahamas, barbados and the Dominion Republic are grate favourites and we continue to feature some really excellent offer s.

uc Find out more by contacting Julie kent at our Head Office or by visiting your local travel agent tomorrow.

Page 57 – section review

1 Correction sign's should always be marked with a different colored pen.

2 Errors could be in punctuation, spelling grammer or layout.

3 all numerical data should be checked for accuracy and any errors or omisions identified.

4 It is preferably that two people check a document one reading and the other checking.

5 Errors should be brought to the attention of the author and amendment if neccesary.

6 The Image of the company can be spoiled by badly presented documents

7 If your spelling is pooor, you should use the spell check on your word proccessor.

8 When typing documents, always read through for error s before taking the page from your typewriter.

9 A dictionery should be used if your spelling is not to good.

10 It is sensible to use a ruler when checking documents containing figures?

3.3 Update records in a computerised database

Page 63 – section review

1 database
2 fields
3 sorted
4 report
5 back up

6 password
7 Data Protection
8 heat
9 connections
10 overwriting

Page 63 – wordsearch

E	X	E	O	Y	U	P	T	L	W	N
B	L	K	H	M	Q	L	T	J	K	P
W	V	E	D	F	T	U	V	D	U
A	C	H	C	O	O	E	T	E	I	K
F	A	U	L	T	S	Z	U	P	S	C
W	Q	P	N	J	R	D	F	G	K	A
E	R	I	R	E	P	O	R	T	O	B
H	R	E	C	O	R	D	N	N	E	W
P	A	S	S	W	O	R	D	I	P	R
V	B	W	R	H	J	I	R	E	C	Q
V	L	Y	D	A	T	A	B	A	S	E

4.1 Process petty cash transactions

Page 64

'Petit' is the French word for small.

Additional items which could be paid out of petty cash
buffet food (inhouse food)
travelling expenses, including petrol and taxi fares
entertaining expenses (taking visitors out)
employees' telephone bills
stationery items
batteries
Post Office fees for special mail
laundry
newspapers and magazines

Page 65

The petty cash voucher acts as a receipt for cash which has been paid from petty cash. The receipt should be kept in the box to assist balancing.

Petty Cash Voucher	No 112 Date 21 May 199-

For what required	Amount £	p
1 Box 5¼ " computer disks	7	20
	7	20

Signature   A. Student
Authorised   A. Tutor

Petty Cash Voucher	No 113 Date 23 May 199-

For what required	Amount £	p
Sandwiches for Directors' lunch meeting	11	50
2 cartons of orange drink	1	90
	13	40

Signature   A. Student
Authorised   A. Tutor

Petty Cash Voucher	No 114 Date 24 May 199-

For what required	Amount £	p
Fee for special delivery letter	2	04
Fee for mailing parcel	5	20
	7	24

Signature   A. Student
Authorised   A. Tutor

Petty Cash Voucher	No 115 Date 25 May 199-

For what required	Amount £	p
Desk polish	2	50
Duster	1	40
	3	90

Signature   A. Student
Authorised   A. Tutor

Page 68

Task 1 £31.74 = £7.24 + £13.40 + £7.20 + £3.90

Task 3 £118.26

Task 4   £30.00
                15.00
                46.00
                24.50
                 1.40
                 0.60
                 0.65
                 0.08
                 0.03
TOTAL £118.26

Page 69 – section review

1 transaction
2 process
3 supported
4 authorised
5 security
6 imprest
7 irregularity
8 recorded
9 analysis
10 procedures

D	F	H	K	W	S	E	C	U	R	I	T	Y	Q
Q	X	T	U	V	D	K	L	A	R	E	T	F	D
N	P	E	T	T	Y	C	A	S	H	I	E	R	T
O	D	V	C	M	I	Y	R	C	R	K	H	B	C
I	D	C	Q	V	H	A	N	A	L	Y	S	I	S
T	Q	C	X	Z	O	K	L	F	Y	W	A	B	O
C	S	I	P	Q	A	U	T	H	O	R	I	S	E
A	N	B	X	P	G	C	C	Q	J	K	D	E	W
S	S	A	F	E	T	Y	C	H	E	T	Y	J	K
N	A	G	R	K	Y	Y	N	U	E	P	L	G	D
A	V	R	Y	N	X	J	M	R	R	R	J	L	U
R	I	M	P	R	E	S	T	F	S	A	D	A	L
T	E	W	D	J	C	O	T	P	A	X	T	T	E
G	B	Q	Y	U	M	L	P	S	Z	F	B	E	T

4.2 Process incoming invoices for payment

Page 74 – invoice calculations

1 £452.38

2 £2357.52

3 £586.91

4 £480.32

5 £6521.66

Page 74 – errors in calculations

Incorrect totals

1 should be £449.44

5 should be £998.75

Page 75 – section review

1 delivery

2 GRN

3 computerised

4 NCR

5 invoices

6 E & OE

7 discount

8 accounts

9 errors

10 authorised

5.1 Stock handling

Page 77 – missing letters

1 A4 bond paper

2 A4 bank paper

3 letter head paper

4 carbon paper

5 card

6 labels

7 envelopes

8 message pads

9 document folders

10 pencils

11 ball point pens

12 correction fluid

13 adhesive tape

14 staplers and staples

15 scissors

16 hole punches

17 rubber stamps

18 bulldog clips

19 paper clips

20 elastic bands

Page 77 – additional consumables

memo paper	graph paper
photocopy paper	index cards
envelopes – all sizes	padded postage bags
floppy disks	disk boxes
folders – all types	tally rolls
fax rolls	daisy wheels
felt-tip pens	erasers
pencil sharpeners	rubber thimbles
Sellotape	drawing pins
string	brown paper
calculator batteries	ink stencils

Page 77 – picture identification

1 paper knife
2 box file
3 paper clip
4 bulldog clip
5 lever arch file
6 hole reinforcement stickers
7 paper punch
8 file clip
9 staple remover
10 typewriter ribbon cartridge
11 spiral-bound notepad
12 computer printout paper
13 diskette box
14 floppy disk
15 typewriter correction ribbon
16 date stamp
17 wallet folder
18 message pad

Page 78

The stock room and stationery cupboard should be kept locked to stop stealing and people helping themselves to stationery which would not be recorded on the stationery record card. The balances in stock would therefore be incorrect.

Page 79

1 Large, bulky items would be difficult to place and retrieve from top shelves.

2 Frequently requested items should be easy to reach, without the need for steps and stools – saves time.

3 If small items were unseen, assumption could be that they were out of stock.

4 Pens and pencils could roll to back or roll off shelves.

5 Old stock items should always be used first. Existing stock could deteriorate or become out of date.

6 Dampness can affect the quality of paper, it can become crinkly, therefore unsuitable for using in photocopier.

Page 80

Georgia Kingston's approval is needed to discourage staff from ordering unnecessary stationery and to prevent pilferage.

STATIONERY REQUISITION

FROM _Mark Greenwood_ DATE _17 Nov 199-_

DEPT _Technical_ REQ NO 731

Please supply:

Quantity	Item
4 pkts	A4 bond paper
1 box	Staples

Signed: ....

Approved by: ....

STATIONERY REQUISITION

FROM _Sarah Longworth_ DATE _17 Nov 199-_

DEPT _Secretarial_ REQ NO 732

Please supply:

Quantity	Item
5 pkts	A4 bond paper
6 bttls	correction fluid
4 reams	A4 letter head paper

Signed: ....

Approved by: ....

STATIONERY REQUISITION

FROM _Hanif Sidat_ DATE _17 Nov 199-_

DEPT _Sales_ REQ NO 733

Please supply:

Quantity	Item
8 pkts	A4 bond paper

Signed: ....

Approved by: ....

STATIONERY REQUISITION

FROM _Jennifer Thomas_ DATE _17 Nov 199-_

DEPT _Admin_ REQ NO 734

Please supply:

Quantity	Item
1 ream	A4 letter head paper
6 bttls	correction fluid
2 boxes	staples

Signed: ....

Approved by: ....

Page 81

1 80 batteries should be ordered to restore maximum balance.
2 Supplier – Summit Lighting Company

Page 82 Stationery record cards

STATIONERY RECORD CARD

ITEM: ....A4 BOND PAPER.................. MAX: 500

SUPPLIER: STOCKTON PAPER COMPANY. MIN: 50

Date	Quantity received	Quantity issued	Dept	Req No	Balance in stock
1 Nov					83
10 Nov		6	Sec	698	77
10 Nov		16	Admin	699	61
17 Nov		4	Tech	731	57
17 Nov		5	Sec	732	52
17 Nov		8	Sales	733	44

STATIONERY RECORD CARD

ITEM: ....CORRECTION FLUID.............. MAX: 100

SUPPLIER: ...OFFICE EQUIPMENT PLC.... MIN: 20

Date	Quantity received	Quantity issued	Dept	Req No	Balance in stock
1 Nov					65
3 Nov		3	Tech	671	62
10 Nov		6	Sec	702	56
17 Nov		6	Sec	732	50
17 Nov		6	Admin	734	44

STATIONERY RECORD CARD

ITEM: ....STAPLES.......................... MAX: 50

SUPPLIER: ..OFFICE EQUIPMENT PLC..... MIN: 10

Date	Quantity received	Quantity issued	Dept	Req No	Balance in stock
1 Nov					18
5 Nov		5	Sec	675	13
17 Nov		1	Tech	731	12
17 Nov		2	Admin	734	10

STATIONERY RECORD CARD

ITEM: ....A4 LETTER HEAD PAPER......... MAX: 300

SUPPLIER: STOCKTON PAPER COMPANY MIN: 50

Date	Quantity received	Quantity issued	Dept	Req No	Balance in stock
1 Nov					56
10 Nov		2	Sec	702	54
17 Nov		4	Sec	732	50
17 Nov		1	Admin	734	49

2 The items which need re-ordering are:

A4 bond paper

staples

A4 letter head paper

Page 83 stationery record cards

STATIONERY RECORD CARD

ITEM: .... A4 BOND PAPER .... MAX: 500

SUPPLIER: STOCKTON PAPER COMPANY. MIN: 50

Date	Quantity received	Quantity issued	Dept	Req No	Balance in stock
1 Nov					83
10 Nov		6	Sec	698	77
10 Nov		16	Admin	699	61
17 Nov		4	Tech	731	57
17 Nov		5	Sec	732	52
17 Nov		8	Sales	733	44
29 Nov	456				500

STATIONERY RECORD CARD

ITEM: .... CORRECTION FLUID .... MAX: 100

SUPPLIER: ...OFFICE EQUIPMENT PLC.... MIN: 20

Date	Quantity received	Quantity issued	Dept	Req No	Balance in stock
1 Nov					65
3 Nov		3	Tech	671	62
10 Nov		6	Sec	702	56
17 Nov		6	Sec	732	50
17 Nov		6	Admin	734	44

STATIONERY RECORD CARD

ITEM: .... STAPLES .... MAX: 50

SUPPLIER: ..OFFICE EQUIPMENT PLC..... MIN: 10

Date	Quantity received	Quantity issued	Dept	Req No	Balance in stock
1 Nov					18
5 Nov		5	Sec	675	13
17 Nov		1	Tech	731	12
17 Nov		2	Admin	734	10
29 Nov	40				50

STATIONERY RECORD CARD

ITEM: ...... A4 LETTERHEAD PAPER .... MAX: 300

SUPPLIER: STOCKTON PAPER COMPANY. MIN: 50

Date	Quantity received	Quantity issued	Dept	Req No	Balance in stock
1 Nov					56
10 Nov		2	Sec	702	54
17 Nov		4	Sec	732	50
17 Nov		1	Admin	734	49
29 Nov	251				300

Page 84

The stationery record cards will show to which departments the stock has been issued.

Page 85 – section review

1 requisition
2 consumable
3 hazardous and inflammable
4 obsolete
5 emergency
6 legislation
7 discrepancy
8 legible and accurate
9 reconciliation
10 manual and computerised

6.1 Receive, sort and distribute incoming/internal mail

Page 88 – Remittances book

REMITTANCES BOOK		DATE ......*Today's date*............			
Name of sender	Method of payment	Amount £	p	Account number	Signature
Calvert Bros	cheque	426	50	67245	A Student
K Higson	cash	80	00	23694	A Student
Paul Banks	cheque	73	96	32463	A Student
Anwar Hussain	cheque	32	80	34895	A Student
P O'Brien	cheque	895	00	12423	A Student
S Anderson	cash	65	00	23574	A Student
T Dickinson	postal order	5	00	43286	A Student

Cashier's signature ....*A Tutor*.......................

Page 89 – section review

1 internal
2 confidential
3 knife
4 envelopes
5 urgent
6 damage
7 sorted
8 routing
9 remittances
10 suspicious

6.2 Prepare for despatch outgoing/internal mail

Page 97 – section review

1 internal
2 enclosures
3 window
4 envelope
5 Parcelforce
6 registered
7 jiffy
8 postage
9 scales
10 cardboard

Page 97 – wordsearch

M	A	I	L	R	O	O	M	L	D	P
D	R	E	H	J	F	D	S	I	E	M
G	V	E	N	H	G	F	R	A	A	A
N	W	Q	G	H	O	J	G	M	D	T
I	F	S	H	I	J	T	A	R	L	S
K	G	J	P	F	S	H	K	I	I	O
N	E	R	H	J	D	T	W	A	N	P
A	D	U	P	L	N	M	E	F	E	A
R	S	W	I	F	T	A	I	R	S	T
F	R	E	E	P	O	S	T	T	E	A
S	D	G	R	E	C	O	R	D	E	D

7.1 Produce copies from original documents using reprographic equipment

Page 99 – photocopying costs

Company A = £185
Company B = £280
Company C = £315

Page 105 – section review

1 copyright
2 metal
3 plain
4 reprography
5 toner

6 trained
7 rental
8 scanner
9 waste
10 fastened

Page 105 – wordsearch

D	B	H	C	U	R	H	W	L	I	T	C
Z	O	F	F	S	E	T	L	I	T	H	O
U	R	G	E	N	T	P	T	N	S	E	P
B	S	T	A	P	L	E	L	E	P	R	Y
C	X	Y	K	S	T	J	N	F	G	M	R
J	M	V	T	A	D	I	P	C	N	A	I
X	K	T	L	K	L	F	R	K	I	L	G
F	D	L	D	D	C	L	O	G	D	L	H
B	O	M	A	F	L	Y	F	F	U	I	T
C	R	E	P	R	O	G	R	A	P	H	Y
K	D	U	P	L	I	C	A	T	I	N	G

8.1 Receive and assist callers

Page 107 – non-verbal communications

1 C
2 D
3 A
4 B

Page 110 – section review

1 greeting
2 delay
3 image
4 introducing
5 security

6 escort
7 difficult
8 appointments
9 confidential
10 register

Page 111 – crossword

```
            ¹I  M  A  G  E        ²B  A  G  S
      ³N                          A
⁴L  O  C  K  E  D                 D              ⁵S
    N                             G               E
    V        ⁶P  O  L  I  T  E                    C
    E         R                                   U
    R         O        ⁷V  I  S  I  T  O  R       R
    B         M                                   I
 ⁸A  P  P  O  I  N  T  M  E  N  T                 T
    L         T                                   Y
```

8.2 Maintain business relationships with other members of staff

Page 113 – organising the workload

Suggested order of tasks

5, 7, 6, 12, 4, 13, 1, 10, 11, 3, 9, 2, 14, 8

Page 115 – section review

1 willingly
2 deadlines
3 appearance
4 communicate
5 workload

6 colleagues
7 uniform
8 apologise
9 title
10 clean

Page 115 – wordsearch

```
H  C  O  L  L  E  A  G  U  E  Y
S  F  G  U  G  K  P  A  D  T  N
G  C  E  A  T  P  O  U  R  T  R
C  X  M  P  U  O  T  U  E  E  C
G  I  B  F  D  L  O  R  S  E  A
G  U  O  G  H  I  K  O  S  R  L
F  S  H  T  V  T  U  R  F  C  L
C  L  E  A  N  E  B  V  H  S  E
F  E  H  T  G  H  R  E  W  I  R
K  E  S  T  A  N  D  A  R  D  S
B  K  U  W  O  R  K  L  O  A  D
```

144 Business Administration: Student Handbook

9.1 Health and safety

Page 116 – identifying hazards

Picture 1	Carrying too many files, fire door propped open
Picture 2	Plug socket overloaded, boiling kettle near edge of table
Picture 3	Sun glare on VDU screen, person stood on swivel chair
Picture 4	Bags lying in aisle, worn carpet
Picture 5	Waste bin being used as ashtray, person licking envelopes to seal
Picture 6	Boxes blocking emergency exit, trailing flex
Picture 7	Papers blowing onto fire, scissors on edge of desk
Picture 8	Carrying heavy equipment, filing cabinet door left open

Page 117 – additional potential hazards

- Smoking in 'no smoking' areas (particularly near flammable materials)
- Bags, articles or equipment left in passageways
- Bringing liquids (coffee, tea) into an electrical area eg computer room
- Boxes stacked too high
- Spillages not cleaned up immediately
- Not using correct stepladders to reach high shelves
- Running down corridors
- Not following manufacturer's instructions when using machinery

Page 117 – reasons for evacuating a building

Practice fire drill   Bomb threat   Gas leak

Page 118 – fire extinguishers

1	red	**5**	cream
2	blue	**6**	cream
3	blue	**7**	black
4	green		

Page 120 – suggested contents of first aid box

- individually wrapped sterile bandages
- sterile eye pads, with attachment
- sterile triangular bandages
- safety pins
- sterile unmedicated dressings (large, medium and small)
- assorted plasters
- cotton wool
- lint
- finger stall
- plastic gloves
- scissors

No drugs should be kept in first aid box!

Page 120 – completed accident report form

ACCIDENT REPORT FORM

Name of injured person MATTHEW KINGSTON	Age 28

Home address   15 TENBY CLOSE BRIDGETOWN

Department   ACCOUNTS

Date of accident	Time 1.15 pm

Where did accident happen?   ON STAIRS OUTSIDE CANTEEN

How did accident occur?   SLIPPED DOWN STAIRS

Details of injuries   BADLY GRAZED BACK AND DISLOCATED THUMB

Details of treatment given at work   TAKEN TO FIRST AID ROOM AND ARM PUT IN SLING

Did the injuries require hospital treatment?   YES

Name of witness to accident   SIMON WALKER

SIGNATURE of person reporting the accident ___ A. Student

DATE ___ Today's date

Page 121 – section review

1 extinguishers
2 HASAWA
3 potential hazards
4 accident book
5 machinery
6 evacuate
7 first aid box
8 bomb threats
9 temperature
10 safety representative

Page 121 – wordsearch

Y	F	S	S	J	V	H	B	K	G	S	W
S	T	L	U	S	W	T	C	P	U	T	N
L	N	I	O	P	O	L	I	C	Y	R	Q
O	E	F	R	A	L	A	R	M	S	U	M
J	D	B	E	O	E	V	K	D	D	L	V
X	I	N	G	K	H	S	F	I	R	E	P
H	C	W	N	Y	E	T	E	G	A	S	I
N	C	H	A	U	M	C	U	O	Z	T	M
Q	A	V	D	J	M	P	J	A	A	C	T
D	F	V	F	P	Q	A	L	U	H	L	C
F	W	G	C	M	O	Q	J	L	Q	Z	M
J	L	P	E	U	X	S	A	F	E	T	Y

File

Index cards

Name	Number		
Address			
Telephone No	Date of birth		
Details			

Name	Number		
Address			
Telephone No	Date of birth		
Details			

Name	Number		
Address			
Telephone No	Date of birth		
Details			

Name	Number		
Address			
Telephone No	Date of birth		
Details			

Absent card

FILE BORROWED	BORROWER'S NAME	DEPARTMENT	DATE BORROWED	DATE RETURNED	OUT

Correction symbols
Mark all errors using correction symbols.

CRUISING

Have you ever considered a cruise for your anual holiday.
There is a magnificent chioce available with prices ranging
from a very modest £495 to 9,995.

Pampered passengers has the choice of superb cuisine, five
resturants, four swimming pools three lounge bars, a theater,
two ballrooms, a disco and a casino.
Such a choice of things todo means that every pasenger can can
enjoy the lifestyle which suites him or her best. You day
could drift lazily past with a quite stroll on deck, a game of
bridge, a piano recital or a lecture from a well-known
personality
on the otherhand, you may preferr to tone up in the health
spa, swing a golf Club, take in a show and then dance under the
stars until another day dawns.

There are big savings for children, as wellas for three or
four adults sharing a room and to have an extra week can cost
as little as £50 per person.
Jamaca, the Bahamas, barbados and the Dominion Republic are
grate favourites and we continue to feature some really
excellent offer s.
Find out more by contacting Julie kent at our Head Office or
by visiting your local travel agent tomorrow.

Suggested employee record for database

EMPLOYEE RECORD

SURNAME _____ FIRST NAME _____ M/F _____

ADDRESS _____

_____

_____ POSTCODE _____

TEL NO _____ DATE OF BIRTH _____

DEPARTMENT _____ DATE JOINED _____

STARTING SALARY _____ DATE LEFT _____

Petty cash vouchers

| Petty Cash Voucher | No _____ |
| | Date _____ |

For what required   Amount
                                   £   p

Signature _____

Authorised _____

| Petty Cash Voucher | No _____ |
| | Date _____ |

For what required   Amount
                                   £   p

Signature _____

Authorised _____

| Petty Cash Voucher | No _____ |
| | Date _____ |

For what required   Amount
                                   £   p

Signature _____

Authorised _____

| Petty Cash Voucher | No _____ |
| | Date _____ |

For what required   Amount
                                   £   p

Signature _____

Authorised _____

Stationery requisitions

STATIONERY REQUISITION

FROM .... DATE ....

DEPT .... REQ NO 731

Please supply:

Quantity	Item

Signed: ....

Approved by: ....

STATIONERY REQUISITION

FROM .... DATE ....

DEPT .... REQ NO 733

Please supply:

Quantity	Item

Signed: ....

Approved by: ....

STATIONERY REQUISITION

FROM .... DATE ....

DEPT .... REQ NO 732

Please supply:

Quantity	Item

Signed: ....

Approved by: ....

STATIONERY REQUISITION

FROM .... DATE ....

DEPT .... REQ NO 734

Please supply:

Quantity	Item

Signed: ....

Approved by: ....

Stationery record cards

STATIONERY RECORD CARD

ITEM: STAPLES MAX: 50

SUPPLIER: OFFICE EQUIPMENT PLC MIN: 10

Date	Quantity received	Quantity issued	Dept	Req No	Balance in stock
1 Nov					18
5 Nov		5	Sec	675	13

STATIONERY RECORD CARD

ITEM: A4 LETTER HEAD PAPER MAX: 300

SUPPLIER: STOCKTON PAPER COMPANY MIN: 50

Date	Quantity received	Quantity issued	Dept	Req No	Balance in stock
1 Nov					56
10 Nov		2	Sec	702	54

STATIONERY RECORD CARD

ITEM: A4 BOND PAPER MAX: 500

SUPPLIER: STOCKTON PAPER COMPANY MIN: 50

Date	Quantity received	Quantity issued	Dept	Req No	Balance in stock
1 Nov					83
10 Nov		6	Sec	698	77
10 Nov		16	Admin	699	61

STATIONERY RECORD CARD

ITEM: CORRECTION FLUID MAX: 100

SUPPLIER: OFFICE EQUIPMENT PLC MIN: 20

Date	Quantity received	Quantity issued	Dept	Req No	Balance in stock
1 Nov					65
3 Nov		3	Tech	671	62
10 Nov		6	Sec	702	56

Page from a remittances book

REMITTANCES BOOK

DATE ....

Name of sender	Method of payment	Amount £	p	Signature

Cashier's signature ....

Fire extinguishers

1 Used for class A fires
e.g wood, cloth, paper.

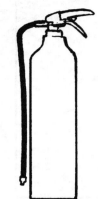

Water

2 Can be used on live
electrical equipment e.g
TV sets, computers.

Multi-purpose dry powder

3 Can also be used on live
electrical equipment.

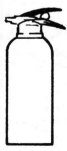

Standard dry powder

4 Ideal for use in
car fires.

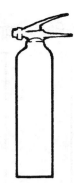

Halon 1211(BCF)

5 Can be used on class
A and class B fires
e.g. furniture fires or
paraffin heaters. More
effective than water.

*AFFF (Aqueous film-forming
foam) (multi-purpose)*

6 Use on class B fires –
a blanket of foam
smothers the flames.

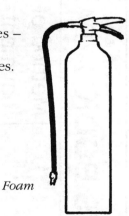

Foam

7 Clean, effective and
safe when used on live
electrical equipment.

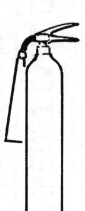

Carbon dioxide (Co2)

Accident report form

ACCIDENT REPORT FORM

Name of injured person	Age

Home address

Department

Date of accident	Time

Where did accident happen?

How did accident occur?

Details of injuries

Details of treatment given
at work

Did the injuries require hospital treatment?

Name of witness to accident

SIGNATURE of person reporting the accident ....

DATE ....

Index

Absent cards	14
Accident book	120
Accounts department	71, 75
Addressing envelopes	91–3
Advice of delivery	94
Airmail	94
Airstream	94
Alphabetical filing	6
Answering machines	21–2
Apostrophes	40–1
Appearance	114, 125
Applying for a job	122–4
Back-up copies	61
Bar charts	32
Binders	103
Bomb threats	24
Business letters	42–4
Business relationships	112–13
Business reply service	94
Callers	106–10
Cash discount	73
Centralised filing	13
Certificate of posting	94
Checking invoices	73
Chronological filing	7
Circulation list	88
Collating equipment	102
Colleagues – liaising with	106–10
Communications – messages	26–9
– non-verbal	107
– verbal	17–24
– written	42–5
Compensation fee parcel	94
Computerised filing systems	58–62
Computerised stock records	84
Computers – database	58–62
– disks	61
– faults	62
– security	62

Confidentiality – callers	109
– computers	62
– enquiries	24
– files	11
– mail	86
– telephone	24
Consumables	76–84
Copying costs	99
Copyright legislation	104
Correction marks	56
Credit notes	70, 74
Crimper	104
Cross-reference cards	10
Curriculum vitae (CV)	122–4
Databases – amending, updating	59
– entering data	59
– records	58
Datapost	94
Data Protection Act	62
Debit notes	70
Delivery notes	70, 71
Difficult – callers	107–8
– colleagues	112–13
Discounts	73
Distribution lists	88
Document retention	11
Dress	114
Duplicating systems	98–104
Electronic filing	59
Enclosures	90
Envelopes	91–3
Equipment – filing	7–12
– fire fighting	117
– mailroom	87
– reprographic	98–104
– typewriters	47
Errors – checking techniques	54
– identifying	54
Escorting callers	108–9
Express delivery	94

Filing – centralised 13
   – cross-referencing 10
   – departmental 13
   – equipment 7
   – retention of documents 11
   – sorting documents 5
   – systems 6–11
See also electronic filing,
computer filing systems, indexing
systems and microfiche
Fire fighting equipment 117
First aid 120
Floppy disks – care of 61
   – copying
     and back-up 61
Franking machines 96
Freefone 23
Freepost 94

Geographical filing 7
Goods received notes (GRN) 71–2
Grammar 35–6
Graphs 32
Grooming 114, 125

Health and Safety – filing 8
   – stock 78
   – workplace 116
Health and Safety at Work Act
 (HASAWA) 118
Histograms 32

Imprest 65
Indexing systems 9–10
Information – abstracting 30
   – deadlines 33
   – presenting 32
   – researching 30
   – sources of 30
Ink duplicating 98
Inserting machines 96
Internal direct dialling (IDD) 23
Interviews 125
Introductions 109
Invoices 70, 72, 73

Job applications 122–4

Keyboard equipment 47–9

Letter delivery offices 30
Letter of enquiry 70
Letter opening machine 87
Letters 42–4
Liaising with callers and
  colleagues 106–10
Line graphs 32

Mail handling – incoming 86–8
   – outgoing 90–6
Mailroom equipment 87, 96
Making telephone calls 20
Memos 44–5
Message taking 26–8
Microfiche 11
Microfilm 11
Multi-page documents 102

Non-verbal communications 107
Numerical filing 7

Office consumables 76–84
Offset litho duplicating 99
Order form 70
Out cards 14

Parcelforce 30, 94
Parcels – postal services 94
   – suspicious 88
   – wrapping 93
Passwords 62
Personal mail 86
Petty cash 64–8
Photocopiers 99–102
Pie charts 32
Postage book 95
Postage scales 96
Post Office Counters Ltd 30, 86
Presenting information 32–3
Prestel 30
Printing data 51
Proof-reading 55–6
Punches 5
Punctuation 39–41
Purchasing department 75

Quotations 70

Receiving goods 71–2
Recorded delivery 94
Reference books 22, 31
Reference libraries 30
Registered post 94
Reminder systems 15
Remittances 87–8
Reprographics 98
Requisitions 79–104
Researching information 30–1
Returns diary 15
Routing slip 88
Royal Mail services 30, 94

Safety – see Health and Safety
Sales Department 75
Security – database 62
– petty cash 64
– telephone 24
– visitors 109
Shredding machine 11
Sources of information 30–1
Special delivery 94
Spell checkers 48
Spelling 37–9
Spirit duplicating 98
Staff relationships 112–13
Stapler 102
Statements 70
Stationery 76–84
Stock – computerised records 84
– consumables 76–84
– issuing 79
– reconciliation 84
– records 80
– re-ordering 82, 104
– requisitions 79
– safety 78
– stock-taking 84
– storage 78, 104
Subject filing 7
Supplying information 30
Suspicious mail 88
Swiftair 94

Telephone – alphabet 20
– answering machines 21–2
– charges 23–4
– confidentiality 24
– emergency calls 24
– faults 23
– features 18
– incoming calls 19–20
– messages 26–9
– outgoing calls 20
– reference books 22
– security 24
– services 23
– systems 17–18
– wrong numbers 20
Teletext 30
Thesaurus 31
TouchTone phones 18
Trade Descriptions Act 83
Trade discount 73
Typewriters – care of 49
– correction of errors 49
– equipment 47

Value Added Tax (VAT) 73
Viewdata 30
Visitors 106–10
Visual display unit (VDU) 48–9
Vocabulary – extending 41

Word processors 48–9
Wraparound 47